Woodworking

Woodworking

A. B. Emary

M

First published 1979 by
THE MACMILLAN PRESS LTD
London and Basingstoke
Associated companies in Delhi Dublin
Hong Kong Johannesburg Lagos Melbourne
New York Singapore and Tokyo

Typeset by Reproduction Drawings Ltd, Sutton, Surrey
Printed by A. Wheaton & Co., Ltd., Exeter

British Library Cataloguing in Publication Data

Emary, Alfred Bethuen
  Woodworking—(Leisure learning).
  1. Woodwork—Amateurs' manuals
  I. Title   II. Series
  684'.08   TT185
  ISBN 0-333-27124-6   ISBN 0-333-22354-3   (Pbk)

Contents

Preface

This book has been produced chiefly for the amateur woodworker who attends evening classes to obtain expert advice and help in the manufacture of items for the home; it is aimed at those who are unable to attend classes but who derive pleasure and relaxation from shaping and working timber. The book has been divided into two parts. The first deals with the theory of woodwork and the second part gives the reader some ideas on which he can base his own designs.

Of the tools needed by the amateur woodworker, only the basic ones have been considered; even so, the list of these is quite considerable. A few portable tools have also been included because these are sometimes available in evening institutes. No book can really teach a person the correct way to use a tool—this comes with practice and from the teacher who can demonstrate its correct use in the classroom. It is with this in mind that only a brief description of each tool and its uses is given. Most of the accessories, such as sawing stools, a bench, etc., can be made by the woodworker himself, resulting in a great saving in money, if not in time.

Timber has become a very expensive material over the last few years, and this, coupled with the desire in most of us to be able to make things, has inspired me to try to help the amateur woodworker. The book helps the reader to fit out his workshop, whether a garage or a garden shed. It helps him to make his garden more attractive, and shows him how to make items of furniture which will add to the comfort inside his home. I hope, too, that it will assist the woodwork teacher in the production of a programme to work to throughout the evening class session, thus avoiding the awkward situation when a student asks 'What do you suggest I make?'

Although I was primarily thinking of woodwork classes when compiling this book, I hasten to say that the woodworker who is unable to attend classes, can, I hope, obtain much help from its pages so that he too will be able to produce any of the items (there are twenty of them) in his own workshop with comparative ease.

Several woodworking accessories described early in the book can be made by the reader provided he has the basic tools also listed in its pages.

Part I

Part]

1

Timber

Most people consider timber to be the ideal material because it is so
versatile. From it we get food, warmth, shelter, medicine, comfort
(in the form of furniture, for instance) and many other things. It is
also a material which is often used wastefully and everyone knows
that it has recently become very expensive. There is every reason,
then, for us to use it in an economical manner and to prevent if from
decaying, as it most certainly will if it is abused and treated
incorrectly.

HARDWOODS AND SOFTWOODS

Timber can be divided into two groups, hardwoods and softwoods,
the former coming from deciduous trees (one exception being holly,
an evergreen) that shed their leaves at the end of the growing season—
the autumn in temperate zones. In tropical regions leaf-fall usually
occurs at the end of the driest part of the year. The seeds of hardwood trees are produced in seed pods or cases. A typical example is
the horse chestnut; this has a green pod bearing protruding spikes,
and containing a seed called a 'conker'!
  Softwoods come, usually, from evergreen trees—those which do
not shed their leaves. (As with hardwoods, there are one or two excep-
tions.) The seeds of softwoods are produced in cones, which open
when they are mature thus allowing the exposed seeds to fall to the
ground.

Common Softwoods

Many softwoods are used in the timber industries. They include
pines, firs and cedars. The amateur woodworker uses only a few of

these, the most common being red or yellow deal, which, to give it its correct name, is Scots pine, but which is also known as European redwood. Parana pine, which comes mainly from South America, and Western hemlock, a Canadian timber, are two other common softwoods.

Red or yellow deal is a very good general-purpose timber, it has good working qualities, and is the softwood timber which you would usually get at the timber merchant's if no preference were specified. Various grades of this timber are obtainable, so if a piece of joinery is to be made, 'joinery quality' should be specified otherwise one may get a poor quality timber with large knots and splits that would only be suitable for rough work.

Parana pine is in quite plentiful supply and it can be obtained in fairly large lengths free from knots. It has two main drawbacks: it splits very easily and is a rather heavy timber. Its working qualities are good.

Western hemlock which is generally used in poorer quality work, is another softwood that a purchaser may be sold by the timber merchant. It is a very inferior timber—one to be avoided if possible. It usually has large knots, these very often being dead knots, and it can appear to be very woolly and lifeless. This timber is definitely not suitable for joinery purposes.

Common Hardwoods

There are many more hardwoods in common use than there are softwoods and they would be too numerous to list here. However, a few have been selected to give the reader some idea of what to buy when colour and texture may be important features.

Oak is a very popular timber especially if it has been cut in a certain manner. (The sawyer at the mill can cut up a log in several ways, depending on the timber. These will be dealt with later). If oak is quarter-sawn (see figure 1.5), the decorative features will be exposed on the wide surfaces of the board. These features are called 'flower' and greatly enhance the value of the timber. Oak is a heavy timber, difficult to plane and work unless the tools are kept very sharp. English oak is usually not very suitable for furniture joinery unless specially selected, but it is ideal in damp positions. Japanese oak is more suitable for joinery items because it is more open-grained, not as dense or heavy, and works more easily with tools. Oak can vary in colour from very light yellow to fairly deep brown.

Teak has been used very extensively over the last twenty years or so and is now beginning to lose its popularity. It is a yellowish-brown timber with a distinct smell and works well with tools although these tend to blunt easily due to mineral deposits in the grain. It has a greasy feel and being ideal for use in damp conditions is often used for work such as garden seats and the like.

Mahogany has for several years been considered to be an 'old-fashioned wood', whatever this may mean, but its popularity will surely return, much sooner than many people think. Of course, there are many so-called mahoganies around; sapele, for instance, is a very good substitute for a true mahogany. The true mahoganies, such as Honduran and Cuban (the latter is now almost unobtainable), are wonderful timbers, rich in colour, red to chocolate-brown, and reasonably easy to work. The substitute mahoganies, too, are excellent timbers, very similar in colour. However, many of them, especially those from Africa, have interlocked grain, making them more difficult to clean up to a smooth unblemished surface.

Manufactured Boards (figure 1.1)

In addition to 'solid' timber boards several manufactured boards are available to the amateur woodworker. The most common size is 2440 mm (8 ft) × 1220 mm (4 ft), although other sizes are readily available.

Plywood (figures 1.1a and b) is the most widely used manufactured board. It is made from three or more thin veneers glued together so that the grain of each veneer is at right angles to those adjacent to it. The product is a board that can be used in many ways and its great advantages are that it is very strong and movement (shrinkage) is so small as to be almost negligible.

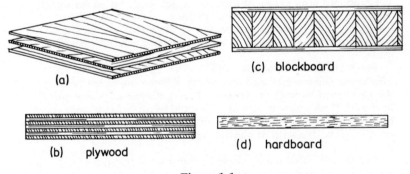

(a)

(c) blockboard

(b) plywood

(d) hardboard

Figure 1.1

Two common grades of plywood are available at timber merchants: *interior* and *exterior*. The latter is weather-resistant and can be used outside the house. Plywood is available in many thicknesses, the most common used by the woodworker being 6 mm ($\frac{1}{4}$ in.) and 9 mm ($\frac{3}{8}$ in.). Plywood can be used for a variety of purposes including door panels, and mould boxes for concrete (exterior grade).

Blockboard (figure 1.1c) is another sheet material in great demand.

The surfaces of blockboard are formed with moderately thin veneers and the core is comprised of strips of wood glued together. Common thicknesses in use are 19 mm ($\frac{3}{4}$ in.) and 12 mm ($\frac{1}{2}$ in.). As with plywood there are differences in the quality of various boards and care should be taken when selecting blockboard to make certain it meets the standard required. For instance, the cheaper board may be twisted or warped or some of the core strips may cause ripples and other irregularities on the board surfaces. Some boards have two good surfaces but others have one good face, and one of only moderate quality.

Table tops and sides to cabinets are among the many applications of blockboard.

Hardboard (figure 1.1d) is made from waste paper and wood-waste. It is inferior to plywood but can be used for many similar purposes. The common thickness is 3 mm ($\frac{1}{8}$ in.) which is very useful for work such as the backs to cabinets, drawer bottoms, etc. As with other boards, hardboard can be purchased in different qualities, the best being 'tempered hardboard', which is reasonably strong compared with the cheaper quality that is little better than cardboard.

Chipboard is made, as its name implies, from wood chips which have been mixed with an adhesive to form a mass. It can be obtained in several thicknesses, the most common being 9 mm, 12 mm and 19 mm. It is purchased in sheet form, the usual size being 2440 × 1220 mm (8 ft × 4 ft). The home woodworker usually buys this material surfaced with a thin plastics covering called melamine.

Chipboard is an excellent material which can be used for many purposes such as shelving, cabinet-making, headboards to beds, wardrobes, etc. It can be purchased in a variety of widths and its edges and ends as well as its face sides, can be surfaced with melamine.

The main drawbacks to melamine-surfaced chipboard are the jointing of the material and its cutting. When a board has been cut the chipboard beneath is exposed. If the cut edge is to be exposed in the finished article it should be treated in one of two ways. It can be filled with a wood filler and painted to match the other surfaces, or covered with a strip of plastics which is secured with a contact adhesive.

In a factory in which chipboard products are manufactured, joining chipboard presents no difficulties because the factory is equipped to deal with this problem. In the home, however, it is another matter. The two pieces to be joined can be glued and nailed, or special screws can be purchased for the work. However, nail or screw holes are hard to hide, especially if melamine-surfaced chipboard is being used. The nail or screw heads can be sunk into the material and specially made plastics plugs can be inserted in the holes. In addition, special ironmongery items can be purchased which assist in the assembly of cabinets and similar work. The fittings may be difficult to find so an alternative method may have to be used.

The most common method for joining two pieces of chipboard at right angles to one another is to use dowels. Accuracy is most essential in this type of joint and this subject is covered later in the book.

Insulating board is another wood-based sheet material which can be used to advantage in the building industry but it does not lend itself to use in the type of work described here. However, if sound insulation is required, one or two thicknesses of 12 mm insulating board, used correctly, will be fairly effective.

Laminated plastics is another sheet material that is used quite extensively at the present time. It is commonly referred to as Formica (a trade name for a specific product). This material can be purchased in a variety of plain colours as well as in a large number of coloured patterns, which include wood grains. Many of the items described in this book may be covered with laminated plastics, especially since hardwoods cost a lot of money. An item made from a comparatively cheap softwood or blockboard can be made to look very attractive when clad in a wood-grain laminated plastics, or, where bathroom fitments are made, in a white plastics. The important thing to remember when applying laminated plastics to the surface of timber is that the contact adhesive must be spread evenly over the two surfaces; when these are perfectly dry the plastics sheet must be placed in position and pressure applied over the whole area by cramps or by a cloth rubber held firmly in the hand.

TREATMENT AND PURCHASE OF TIMBER

Drying

Timber, especially solid timber used for joinery work, should be dry, and if the dryness does not match that of the room in which it is to be placed, the timber will move (shrink or expand), twist or even split, ruining the appearance of the work. Most of the joinery-quality timber bought at a timber merchant's will be fairly dry, but if a very special job is to be carried out and the timber is suspected of having too much moisture within its cells, it should be stacked correctly in a cool to warm atmosphere (preferably in the room in which it will be placed later), so that the moisture content will reach a level which will be equal to that of the room. The method for stacking the timber is shown in figure 1.2.

Sealing

It is important to remember that, having brought the timber to the required moisture content, it should be sealed immediately, or as soon as possible—usually when the item has been completed—to

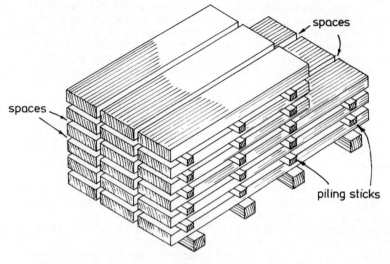

Figure 1.2

reduce any further movement to a minimum. This can be done by coating the timber with one of the following materials: paint, varnish, french polish, or a modern liquid such as polyurethane.

Conversion of Logs

When logs are cut up at the sawyer's they can be converted into boards in one of three ways, namely, through and through (figure 1.3), tangentially (figure 1.4), or quartered (figure 1.5). The first

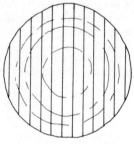

through & through

Figure 1.3

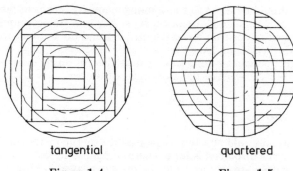

tangential   quartered

Figure 1.4   Figure 1.5

method produces boards which are more suited to rough or carpentry work; some boards may be as shown in figure 1.6a, others may be a little more like those in (b) and (c). The second method would produce boards such as that seen in (b) and the quarter-sawn boards would all be like that shown in (c).

Unfortunately, most of the timber at a merchant's will be from logs cut by the through and through method, so if possible look for boards with the growth rings running in the direction shown in figure 1.6c (preferably) or as in (b). Because timber shrinks in the direction of the growth rings it is easy to see why quarter-sawn boards are more suitable for joinery purposes.

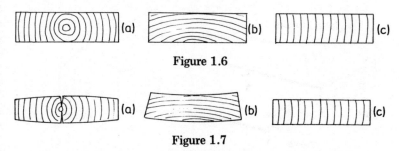

Figure 1.6

Figure 1.7

Figures 1.7a, b and c show what happens to the three types of boards when they shrink. That in (c), the quarter-sawn board, remains reasonably flat.

Allowing Movement

Because all timbers will move slightly with the change of moisture in the atmosphere it is often necessary to make allowances in the construction of solid timber joinery items so that the timber can move without the occurrence of splitting and distortion. For instance, wide table-tops should be fixed to the framing below by means of what are known as shrinkage plates or buttons. Panels in frames should never be glued in position but assembled dry and the battens holding wide boards flat should have their screw holes slotted. These are just three things that can be done to stop degrades appearing in good joinery work as a result of the movement of timber.

Buying Timber

Timber is usually sold at a timber merchant's by the metre run. This means the price displayed is for a length of 1 m, so if, say, 5 m of a particular batten are required and the price displayed is 15 p per metre run, then the price for 5 m will be $15 \times 5 = 75$ p.

Planed or Sawn Timber?

Planed or prepared timber will naturally be more expensive than sawn timber so if a planing machine is available at the evening centre there will be a considerable saving if the sawn boards are purchased and then planed on the machine (or by hand!) at a later time. However, closer inspection is called for if sawn boards are purchased, since defects such as splits or surface checks may be partially hidden when the board is in a sawn state.

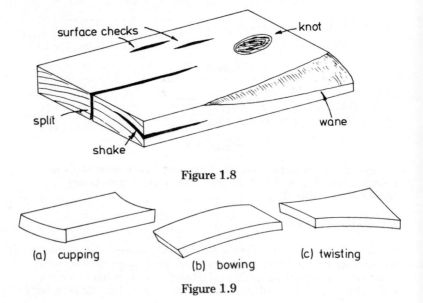

Figure 1.8

(a) cupping   (b) bowing   (c) twisting

Figure 1.9

Defects in Timber

In any case, whether the timber is planed or not, defects such as splits, checks, shakes and knots should be avoided if at all possible (see figure 1.8). These degrades can affect the appearance of a piece of work to a very great extent.

Other defects to be avoided are cupping, twisting and bowing (see figure 1.9). Before purchasing a piece of timber, handle it and sight it through to ensure that it is flat and straight.

Figure in Timbers

Some timbers are more attractive if cut tangentially, and others if they are produced from a log which has been converted to produce quarter-sawn boards. For instance, teak, elm and walnut should be cut tangentially so that the growth rings will show up to advantage on the wide surfaces of the boards (figure 1.10a). Other timbers should be cut in the quarter-sawn fashion to produce attractive features, for example oak (flower) and sapele (stripe) (figure 1.10b).

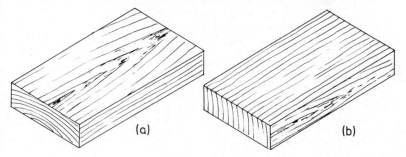

(a)   (b)

Figure 1.10

Metric Dimensions

Some readers may still not be conversant with metric dimensions, so below are a few imperial measurements with their approximate metric equivalents.

1 in.	=	25 mm (25.4)
12 in.	=	300 mm
40 in. (39.37)	=	1000 mm or 1 m

Timber Stock Sizes

The following is a list of the stock sizes in which timber is obtainable. Imperial dimensions and their metric equivalents are given.

$$2 \times 1 \text{ in.} = 50 \times 25 \text{ mm}$$
$$3 \times 2 \text{ in.} = 75 \times 50 \text{ mm}$$
$$4 \times 2 \text{ in.} = 100 \times 50 \text{ mm}$$
$$6 \times 1\tfrac{1}{2} \text{ in.} = 150 \times 38 \text{ mm}$$
$$8 \times 1\tfrac{1}{4} \text{ in.} = 200 \times 32 \text{ mm}$$
$$8 \times 4 \text{ ft} = 2440 \times 1220 \text{ mm}$$

Buying Sheet Materials

Sheet materials are sold by the square metre. A sheet of 2440 × 1220 mm blockboard, for instance, will contain 32 square feet and approximately 3.55 square yards.

2

Tools Required for Home Woodwork

If tools are carefully chosen it is surprising how small a tool kit can be to fulfil the usual requirements of the average household. It is not the purpose of these notes to try to explain the correct way to use tools—this is best done in the workshop at the school in which the woodwork classes are held, where they can be demonstrated correctly. Let us just make a list of what are considered essential tools.

Handsaw Since little sawing needs to be done in the home it is considered best to purchase a panel saw which is likely to prove more useful than a rip saw or a cross-cut saw. This is in the form of a hand-saw and can be used for cross-cutting, ripping, cutting tenons, and most general sawing work. A saw which will be in constant use is the *tenon saw*. This is used for many purposes, such as cutting shoulders to many types of joint, dovetailing, trimming off lengths of timber, mitring, etc.

Metal smoothing plane Record or Stanley makes are suggested. This is an important tool in the kit and should be kept in a good state of repair. It can be used for many purposes including chamfering and bevelling, but its main functions are to prepare a flat surface or to clean up a piece of assembled joinery.

Marking and mortice gauges These are for marking cut lines along the length of a piece of timber in the direction of the grain. The marking gauge has a single tooth so it will mark a single line on the material, whereas the mortice gauge has two teeth, the distance between them being adjustable; thus two parallel cut lines can be marked on the timber at any reasonable distance apart. The marking gauge is used for marking the edges of rebates, mouldings, etc., and the mortice gauge is used for marking mortices, tenons, grooves, and so on—in fact for marking any pair of lines which run parallel to one another.

A try square is a must and is used for marking lines at right angles to the edges of pieces of timber, such as the shoulders to tenons and the ends of mortices, and for marking off timber to length.

Marking knife Although many woodworkers do not use this tool it is considered by the author to be essential if the joints between pieces of timber are to be as near to perfect as possible. The shoulders of tenons should always be marked with a marking knife and the shoulders to halving joints and so on should also be marked with a cut line. Pencil lines can sometimes be very thick, destroying the required accuracy which can be obtained only with a cut line.

Sliding bevel This might be considered similar to a try square but with the sliding bevel the blade of the tool is adjustable, making it possible to mark different angles on the surface of the wood.

Firmer and bevel edged chisels The former of these is used for general purpose work. The latter is useful in operations which require a reasonably good finish; this type is used in the removal of waste from joints involving bevelled shoulders, etc.

Hammer Although joiners use the Warrington-type hammer, the claw hammer is considered the best for someone who will be doing a wide variety of jobs. A couple of nail punches, one for nails such as panel pins and another for larger nails, are also necessary in the kit.

Although the claw hammer is usually sufficient for removing nails from timber it is likely that on the odd occasion a pair of *pincers* will be needed. A piece of plywood or hardboard should always be placed underneath the hammer or pincers when removing a nail, so that the surface of the wood is not damaged.

Brace and twist bits These are for drilling in wood holes that cannot be made with morse drills (see below). They are expensive items and so the woodworker must choose his twist bits to suit the work he will be doing. When purchasing a brace it is well worth the extra expense of buying one with a ratchet, since it is not always possible to turn the brace to its full sweep. A counter-sunk bit for sinking the heads of screws below the surface of the timber is also a necessity.

Wheel brace and morse drills are used mostly for drilling screw holes in timber. There are many sizes of morse drill available but if only a few can be purchased the sizes to obtain should be 2 mm, 3 mm and 6 mm. These should be sufficient for most purposes. When purchasing morse drills it is advisable also to purchase carbon-tipped drills to suit numbers 6, 8, 10 and 12 screws. These will enable the woodworker to drill into brickwork, concrete and other hard materials. It is also as well to remember that pilot holes should be drilled for wire nails and large oval brads (see chapter 6), to prevent splitting the wood.

Another tool which is most useful in the home is one which will enable curves to be cut. This tool is called the *coping saw*. The blades are easily broken if not used carefully but they are fairly cheap to purchase.

Two expensive tools, which are, however, necessary to the home woodworker, are the *metal rebate plane* and the *metal grooving plane*. The main purpose of the rebate plane is to cut rebates in the edges of timber so that glass or panels can be inserted into frames after they have been assembled. The grooving plane is for cutting grooves in timber into which panels can be placed. These tools can be used for other purposes in addition to those mentioned but their main functions are those stated.

3

Joints

Pieces of timber can be nailed or screwed together, they can be glued
to form a join, or they can be jointed together by shaping them in
such a way that they will fit neatly together. When shaped and fitted
together it is usual also to use one of the other forms of jointing, that
is, nailing or screwing and/or gluing, and the result will be a strong
and rigid connection between the timbers.

There are many joints by which timbers can be connected, some
very simple, others more complicated. It is the purpose of this
chapter to give the reader a good idea of some of the joints used in
joinery and furniture-making and to assist him in the problem of
which joint to use for a particular job and also of how the joint
should be constructed. Figures 3.1a and b show two very simple

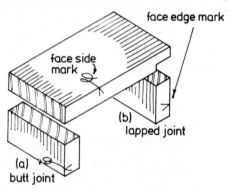

Figure 3.1

joints that are used for jointing two pieces of timber to form a right
angle. The butt joint (a) is formed simply by butting two pieces of
timber together; the important thing, of course, is to get the two
ends to be joined perfectly square. This can be done by carefully

marking the ends with a try square and marking knife and preparing
the ends with a sharp smoothing plane.

Before marking out timber for jointing remember to place on each
piece face side and face edge marks, so that the two pieces will be
assembled in the correct way, and in order to indicate on which
surface further work must be done. In this way mistakes which
would render useless some of the work already done will not be
made.

The lapped joint (b) requires that one of the pieces to be joined
be rebated across the position where the second piece is to fit. This
preparation should be marked out with a marking gauge, try square
and marking knife and the surplus timber removed with tenon saw,
mallet and chisel.

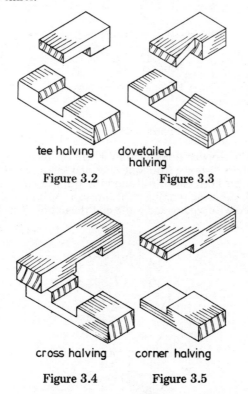

tee halving   dovetailed
            halving
Figure 3.2   Figure 3.3

cross halving   corner halving

Figure 3.4   Figure 3.5

Four halving joints are shown in figures 3.2, 3.3, 3.4 and 3.5.
These joints are used in a variety of jobs and involve removing half
the thickness of the timber from each piece so that their top and
lower surfaces will be flush when fitted. Each joint must be carefully
marked out using a try square and knife for the shoulders and a

gauge for the depth of the recesses; the surplus timber is removed by means of a tenon saw, a mallet and a chisel. The name of each of the joints indicates the type of joint, the dovetailed halving, of course, being the exception. However, this is similar to the tee halving but produces the stronger of the two joints. Figures 3.6a and b show two similar joints which can be used for work such as shelves in cabinets.

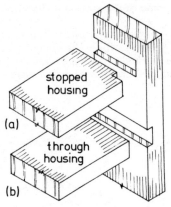

Figure 3.6

At (a) is seen the stopped housing joint where the recess has been terminated a short distance from one edge and the piece which fits into the recess has been cut to fit round the stopped end. The other joint (b) has the housing running right through. Again the shoulders must be marked with square and knife and the depth of each housing marked with a gauge.

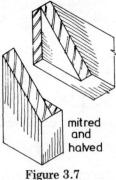

Figure 3.7

Figure 3.7 shows a mitred and halved joint—useful where a strong joint between two timbers is required; this type of joint resembles a mitred joint on the front surfaces. The halved portion of the joint is

fairly simple to mark out but special care must be taken to obtain
accuracy in the mitred portion. Preparation of the joint can be
carried out by means of a tenon saw, and the mitred edges can be
carefully pared with a sharp chisel.

Figures 3.8 to 3.11 show different types of dowelled joint and
steps in their preparation. These joints are now used extensively
perhaps because of the ease with which machines in a factory can
produce them. They are very simple joints but unless extreme care
is taken in marking out and preparation, problems will be encount-
ered which will be difficult to overcome.

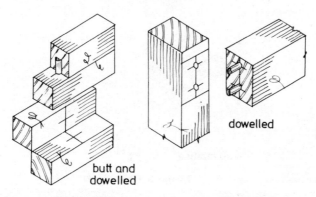

butt and
dowelled

dowelled

Figure 3.8   Figure 3.9

Figure 3.8 shows a butt and dowelled joint; this should be stronger
than the simple butt joint. The two boards to be joined are planed
straight so that their edges are true and the positions of the dowels
are carefully marked on both edges as shown in the figure. The drilling of the holes must be done with care if a good job is to result.
Figure 3.9 shows a dowelled joint. In furniture making this has taken

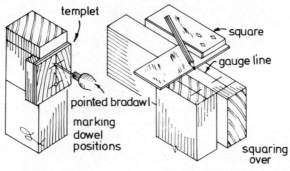

templet

square

gauge line

pointed bradawl

marking
dowel
positions

squaring
over

Figure 3.10   Figure 3.11

the place of the mortice and tenon joint. If the home woodworker is to use this joint he should provide himself with a templet (figure 3.10) to obtain the positions of the dowel holes. The templet can be used on both pieces to be joined.

The method seen in figure 3.11 can also be used for marking out a dowelled joint. The pieces are secured in a vice and by using a gauge and a try square the positions of the dowel holes in each piece can be accurately marked.

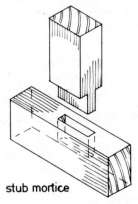

stub mortice

Figure 3.12

The simplest of the mortice and tenon joints is the stub mortice and tenon, (figure 3.12). In this the mortice is allowed to pass through only a portion of the timber into which it is cut. The tenon on the end of the other piece is cut so that it is slightly shorter than the depth of the mortice. This joint is useful where a vertical piece in a framing (called a muntin) is positioned between two rails. The mortice and the tenon should be marked with a mortice gauge and the knife used to mark the shoulders to the tenon.

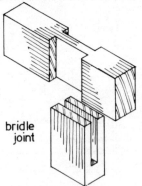

bridle joint

Figure 3.13

The bridle joint seen in figure 3.13 is also called an open mortice and tenon joint and can be used in circumstances similar to those in which the stub mortice and tenon joint is used. The joint should be marked out with mortice gauge, square and knife. The tenon saw, chisels and mallet can be used for removing the surplus timber.

The bridle and dowelled joint (figure 3.14) more or less explains itself and is used where three timbers in a framework intersect at a point. The bridle joint is first assembled and then the holes for the dowels can be drilled after which the third component can be added to the assembly.

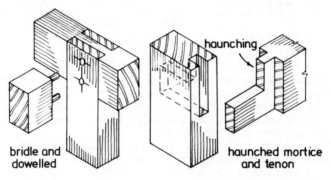

bridle and dowelled

haunching

haunched mortice and tenon

Figure 3.14   **Figure 3.15**

Figure 3.15 shows a haunched mortice and tenon joint which is used at the corner of a piece of framing. The tenon should be the same width as the haunching to prevent weaknesses occurring in either of the two pieces forming the joint. The haunching needs to be only a few millimetres in length, say 10 mm, since its purpose is to prevent the rail from twisting out of position. There are several methods of securing the joint when it has been assembled. These include gluing and wedging, a method which means that provision must be made for a wedge to be glued and inserted on each side of the tenon from the back and driven in with a hammer; alternatively the joint can be secured with a dowel passing through (which will result in the face of the work being spoiled) or a screw can be driven in from the rear (this is acceptable if the back of the frame is hidden from view). Figure 3.16 illustrates a haunched mortice and tenon joint involving the use of a rebate in each piece. For the joint to fit correctly, the tenon shoulder on the same side as the two rebates will have to be allowed to run beyond the shoulder on the other side for a distance equal to the depth of the rebates (see drawing). Figure 3.17 shows another mortice and tenon joint, this time involving a groove in each piece. It shows the marking out required for the mortice and illustrates that allowance has to be made for the groove in the piece containing the tenon.

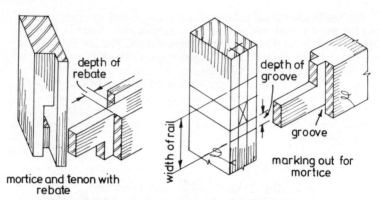

depth of
rebate

depth of
groove

groove

width of rail

marking out for
mortice

mortice and tenon with
rebate

Figure 3.16

Figure 3.17

Figure 3.18 shows another mortice and tenon, in this instance involving rebates and mouldings. If the rebates and the mouldings are exactly the same depth, the allowances on the shoulders will also be exactly the same. The drawing also shows how the mouldings are scribed together at their intersection.

Figures 3.19a, b and c show three methods of making curved components on pieces of work. The first (a) shows that the part has been cut out from a solid piece of timber; this will probably mean that the grain will run across the tenon in a diagonal direction which will result in weakness. A false tenon should therefore be inserted in such a way that its grain will run in the horizontal direction. At (b) is shown a laminated component, made up of a number of thin flexible veneers bent round a former and glued together. This method will be discussed in Part II of this book. The third method (c) shows that a semicircular component has been built up from three thicknesses of timber. They have all been glued and screwed together with the joints staggered. When building up this member, the work should be done on the flat surface on which the required curve has been marked, to enable the correct shape to be obtained.

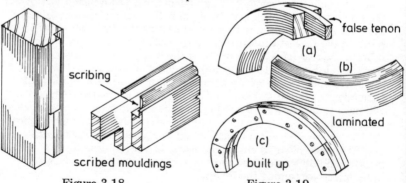

scribing

false tenon

(a)

(b)

laminated

(c)

scribed mouldings

built up

Figure 3.18

Figure 3.19

Probably the most difficult joint to prepare successfully is the dovetailed joint. In furniture work, lapped dovetailed joints are still used quite extensively but they are of course produced on a dovetailing machine or spindle. However, the home woodworker may have to make some of these joints by hand so it is the purpose of these notes and the drawings in figures 3.20a to e to encourage him to attempt this joint so that he will realise it is not such an impossibility as it might appear.

Figure 3.20a is a pictorial view of the completed lapped dovetailed joint; part A might, for example, be the front portion of a drawer to a cabinet or chest of drawers and part B one of its sides. Figures 3.20b and c show how the two parts are marked out. Dimension y (b) must be equal to the thickness of part B and dimension x (c) must be equal to x in (b). This dimension is usually about 5 mm less than the thickness of part A. Before carrying out the marking described it must be borne in mind that the two pieces forming the joint must be perfectly square on their ends. This should be done by first marking the ends with a square and knife and squaring the ends down to the cut lines with a sharp smoothing plane, after which the

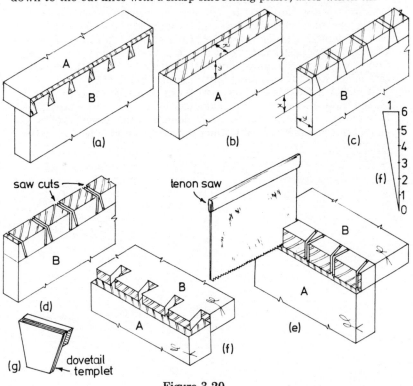

Figure 3.20

marking out previously described can be carried out. The line across
the end of part A should be made by means of a marking gauge, and
the other line on A and that on B should be marked using a square
and a knife.

The dovetails should now be marked on part B as in (c) and to do
this a dovetail templet (g) should be made, with its sides inclined at
an angle of 1 in 6—see (f). An attempt should be made to make all
the dovetails exactly the same size, with the pins somewhat smaller.
When this has been done the dovetail lines should be squared across
the end of part B.

Next, secure the piece B in the vice and with a tenon saw cut
down the outside of the edges of the dovetails, as shown in (d). Then,
with part A secured in the vice and part B laid across the top of A as
shown in (e), using a tenon saw—also seen in the drawing—the marks
to form the pins on part A should be made by applying pressure on
the saw and drawing it through the saw-cut to make the mark required. From the marks thus obtained the pins can be marked on the
end of part A and squared down to the shoulder line seen in (b).

The joint can now be prepared by removing the surplus timber
between the dovetails, part B, with a small bevelled-edge chisel and
mallet, and then removing the surplus timber between the pins,
part A, by using a tenon saw as far as possible and finishing off with
a bevelled-edge chisel and mallet. Be sure, when finishing the preparation of the joint, to remove any small pieces of wood in the recesses
that might stop the two pieces fitting neatly together.

If part A is fixed in the vice, part B can be placed in position as in
(f) and tapped together with a hammer, using a piece of scrap timber
between joint and hammer to avoid damage. If this procedure is
carried out in a methodical manner the joint should appear as in (a).

4

Accessories

There are many aids that the home woodworker can make himself which will greatly help him in the manufacture of many items of carpentry and joinery. The most important of these, of course, is a workbench (figure 4.1). All that is required to make a reasonably good bench is a top, which should be 38–50 mm in thickness, preferably of a hardwood such as beech; two frames made from 75 × 75 mm and 75 × 50 mm timbers, to form the legs; and two 150 × 32 mm boards to make the bench rigid. The size of the bench can be made according to preference, the larger the better, naturally, but if room to accommodate a bench 2 m long by 600 mm wide by 900 mm high is available, this will be found adequate for most jobs. The woodworker can construct cupboards in the space below the bench which will prove invaluable for storage purposes.

The legs and rails are morticed and tenoned together, and are glued with a resin adhesive and dowelled, the dowel sizes being in the region of 12 mm in diameter. The two side boards which help to give the bench its rigidity are recessed into the sides of the leg frames and glued and screwed into position. A 50 × 38 mm crosspiece, the end of

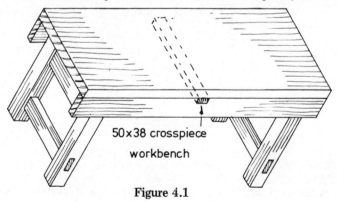

50×38 crosspiece

workbench

Figure 4.1

which can be seen in figure 4.1, should be fixed across the side boards to give support to the centre of the bench top. The top should be fixed by means of stout screws or coach screws, with their heads recessed and the holes filled. A bench vice, if purchased, should be fitted to the bench following the maker's instructions. The sawing stool (figures 4.2a, b and c) is almost indispensable to the home woodworker—in fact, two of these are required. They are used for such purposes as placing timber for sawing and items for assembly. They should be around 700 mm long and of a height according to particular requirements (but probably somewhere around 600 mm).

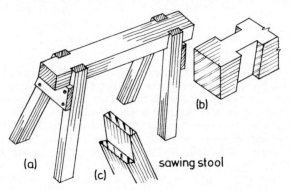

(a) (b) (c) sawing stool

Figure 4.2

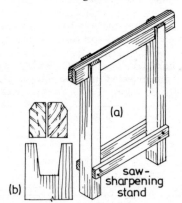

(a) (b) saw-sharpening stand

Figure 4.3

The top, which is recessed at each end as in (b), should be about 75 × 50 mm in size, and the legs, which are prepared as at (c), should be around 50 × 50 mm. The saw-sharpening stand or vice seen in figures 4.3a and b is useful only if the woodworker intends to sharpen his own saws. It has two feet connected to two battens near to the bottom, and the feet are shaped as in (b) at their top ends. Two pieces of timber, bevelled on one of their corners, are cut in such a way as to tighten up together when they are placed in the top ends of the legs—see (b). This action will enable the saw, which is placed between the top battens, to be held firmly so that sharpening can take place.

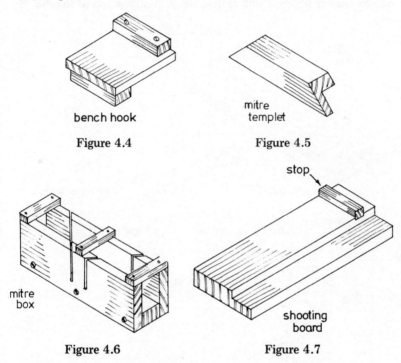

bench hook

Figure 4.4

mitre templet

Figure 4.5

stop

mitre box

Figure 4.6

shooting board

Figure 4.7

The bench hook (figure 4.4) can be used for cross-cutting small pieces of timber with a tenon saw. The hook is placed against the edge of the workbench and the piece of timber against the top batten, enabling the wood to be cut and held firmly.

The mitre templet (figure 4.5) is used for cutting small mitres accurately. The timber should be placed in a vice and the templet placed over a corner so that its mitred end is positioned over the moulding to be mitred; then, with the mitred surface of the templet held firmly in the moulding, the mitre can be formed by slicing off the surplus timber with a sharp chisel.

The mitre box (figure 4.6) is used for cutting mitres on the ends of pieces of timber with a saw. The drawing adequately shows how the box is made.

The two shooting boards shown in figures 4.7 and 4.8 are not so necessary as the other accessories mentioned but are useful on occasions. The shooting board (figure 4.7) can be used for shooting (planing to a straight edge) small lengths of timber with a sharp jack plane. The mitre shoot (figure 4.8) is used for finishing accurately a large mitre on the end of a piece of timber. In each case the plane is placed on its side in the rebate and is pushed along, its cutter slicing off the timber which is held against the stop on the top of the shoot.

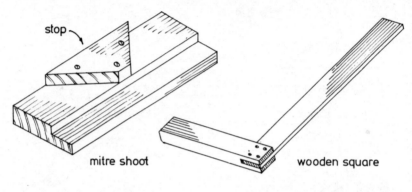

Figure 4.8   Figure 4.9

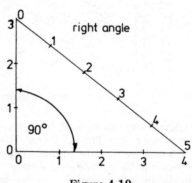

Figure 4.10

Another useful item to have available is a large wooden square similar to that shown in figure 4.9. It can easily be made by joining two pieces of timber by means of an open mortice and tenon joint secured with resin glue and brass screws. Figure 4.10 shows how to check the square from time to time by a method based on the ratio 3:4:5.

5

Terms Applied to Woodwork

There are several terms with which the woodworker should acquaint himself because these appear frequently in most books that deal with woodwork. For instance, a piece of squared timber has four arrises. The term *arris* refers to each sharp corner on the timber (see figure 5.1). Sharp corners or arrises are usually removed by running a sharp smoothing plane once or twice along the corner.

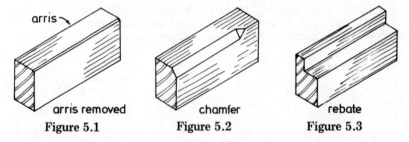

arris		
arris removed	chamfer	rebate
Figure 5.1	**Figure 5.2**	**Figure 5.3**

The removal of an arris must not be confused with making a *chamfer* (figure 5.1). A chamfer is a flat surface usually inclined at 45° and is considerably larger than a slope made by the removal of an arris. Chamfers can be stopped in a manner similar to that shown in figure 5.2.

A *rebate* (figure 5.3) is a recess made along the edge of a piece of wood. It has many uses and is often used in glazed doors and windows. To prepare a rebate an adjustable metal rebate plane should be used. This type of plane can be adjusted to cut a rebate to a required width and depth.

A *groove* is a recess made in or near to the centre of a piece of timber, as shown in figure 5.4. It is used mainly for fitting panels into; however, it has other uses including its part in tongued and grooved joints. The *tongue* of such a joint is made by rebating a piece of timber on two edges as shown in figure 5.5. The groove is best

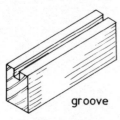
groove
Figure 5.4

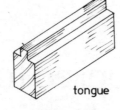
tongue
Figure 5.5

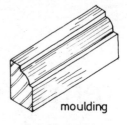
moulding
Figure 5.6

prepared by using an adjustable grooving plane and the tongue by employing a rebate plane.

A *moulding* is a decorative shape often applied to a corner of a piece of wood, as shown in figure 5.6. This can be done in several ways using a moulding plane. A moulding can also be worked along the edge of a piece of timber freehand with a sharp chisel, but this is a tedious method which should only be adopted if no other means are available. If a spindle moulding machine or a portable electric router is available, either of these machines can deal with a moulding job in a very easy and straightforward fashion.

A *bevel* is a surface or end of a piece of timber which has been cut at an angle other than 90° to the other sides or edges (figure 5.7). (Another example of a bevel is shown in figure 5.9a, where two timbers have been bevelled to form a mitre joint.)

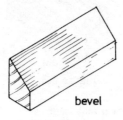
bevel
Figure 5.7

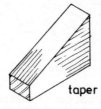
taper
Figure 5.8

mitre (a)

scribe (b)

Figure 5.9

A *taper* is shown in figure 5.8, which shows a piece of timber prepared so that two opposite sides of the piece gradually converge on one another.

Figures 5.9a and b show a *mitre* (a) and a *scribe* (b). These two terms are applied to the joints where two shaped timbers are joined in such a way that the moulded portion of one will fit exactly against the other so that no irregularities occur. Whenever possible, the scribed joint should be chosen because, where shrinkage takes place, the mitred joint can open and spoil the appearance of the work. It must, however, be pointed out that scribing cannot always be carried out because of the nature of the shaped surfaces. In cases such as this mitring must be used.

6

Fixings

Nails and screws play a large part in the fixing of timber. The more common types are shown in figures 6.1a to g.

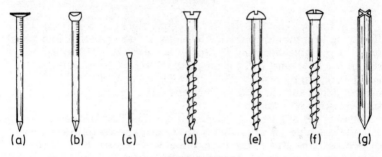

Figure 6.1

The nails shown are the common wire nail (a) the oval brad (b) and the panel pin (c). The first can be used for work of a general nature, the second, the oval brad (b), is a joiner's nail and is used for many types of work where pieces of wood are nailed together; the panel pin (c) is also a joiner's nail and is used for finer work.

A star nail is shown at (g). This can be driven into two pieces of timber forming a joint such as a mortice and tenon, and will assist in holding the joint together.

Three common screws in use today are the *countersunk screw* (d) which, again, is a general-purpose screw used for all kinds of carpentry and joinery work. If deeply countersunk, the heads can be screwed below the timber surface and the holes filled. The *round-head screw* (e) is used where the screw heads are exposed to view and where a countersunk screw would not give the required appearance. The *raised head screw* (f), usually made from brass or some other non-ferrous metal, is a more expensive screw than the other two types but its appearance is more attractive. It is often used in good quality work for such purposes as fixing glazing beads. Its head is partly sunk, making necessary the use of a countersunk bit, and its top edge stands up above the surface of the timber.

Remember to drill pilot holes in the timbers to be nailed or screwed together in order to prevent splitting and also to make the task of turning the screw so much easier. Figure 6.2 shows the various stages in preparing two pieces of timber to receive a countersunk screw.

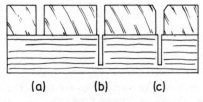

(a)   (b)   (c)

Figure 6.2

When fixing items to brickwork, breeze blocks or concrete, a Rawlplug tool should be used. Alternatively, a tipped drill in a wheel brace or portable electric drill can be used and the hole drilled; the size of the hole must suit the plug and the screw. Numbers 6, 8, 10 and 12 are common sizes. When the hole has been drilled to the correct depth and the plug inserted the screw can be entered and turned with a screwdriver.

Three types of glue are in common use. The first is Resin W, essentially a glue for work that is not to be exposed to the effects of weather. The glue to use for external work should be a synthetic resin, such as Cascomite. This is in powder form and for use must be mixed with water. The third type is a contact glue for gluing laminated plastics to wood. This can be purchased in liquid or jelly form— the jelly type allows for positioning the materials before the pressure is applied.

7

Simple Practical Geometry

Geometry plays a major part in the design and the setting out of items so it is the purpose of this chapter to select a few simple problems involving geometry in the hope that this may assist the reader, in one way or another, to overcome problems in setting out his work.

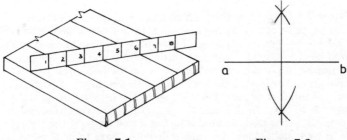

Figure 7.1   Figure 7.2

Figure 7.1 shows a method commonly used for dividing a board into any number of parts, all equal in width. Let us suppose a board is to be divided into four equal widths. Place a rule across the board so that the markings on the rule are in such a position as to make it possible to divide the length of the rule actually on the board into four parts. For instance, the rule in the drawing has been placed over the board so that one of its ends is immediately over one edge of the board and part 8 is over the other edge. Eight can be divided into four quite easily so a mark is made on the board every two sections along the rule, thus enabling parallel lines to be drawn which divide the board into four equal strips.

Figure 7.2 shows how to divide a line into two equal portions. Draw the line a–b and with compass point in each end in turn describe arcs above and below a–b. Then, draw the dividing line through the arcs.

Figure 7.3 shows how an octagon can be drawn to fit into a square of any size. First draw the square a–b–c–d and draw its diagonals a–c and b–d. Place the compass in each corner of the square in turn, and with radius a–x describe the four arcs to give points 1–8 which are the positions of the corners of the octagon.

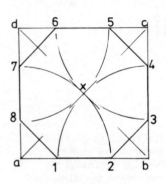

Figure 7.3   Figure 7.4

Figure 7.4 shows a method which can be adopted to draw a regular polygon of any number of sides; in this case a pentagon (with five sides) has been constructed. First, draw the base line a–b to the desired length, extend it along towards point o and with the point of the compass in point a and radius a–b draw the semicircle b–o. Then, by trial and error, divide the semicircle into a number of parts, all equal, the number of parts being equal to the number of sides the polygon is to have. In this case the polygon is to have five sides so the semicircle has been divided into five equal parts. If the polygon were to have eight sides the semicircle would have to be divided into eight equal parts. Draw the second side of the polygon to point 2. Whether the polygon is to have five, six or any other number of sides, the second side of the figure is always drawn from point a to 2.

Then bisect the distances a–b and a–2: the bisecting lines will intersect to give point x. To bisect line a–b place the point of the compass in point a and with it open any distance make an arc above and below the line a–b. Then, with compass point in b and open the same distance, make arcs above and below a–b as before. Draw a line through the intersection of arcs to divide line a–b into two equal parts. This is what is termed 'bisecting a line'. When the bisecting has been done (figure 7.4), place the compass point in x and with radius x–a describe a circle to pass through b–a–2. This is the circle into which the polygon will just fit. Draw a line from point a through 3 to give the top corner of the polygon on the circle and another one from point a through 4 to give the remaining corner. Join up the various points to give the required polygon.

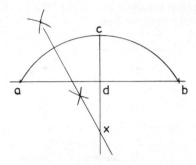

Figure 7.5

Figure 7.5 shows how to construct a segment of a circle when the length of the chord a–b and the height of the curve c–d are given. Draw the chord a–b and bisect it to give point d. From d and on the bisecting line mark the distance d–c. Now bisect a–c and draw the bisecting line to give point x on the centre line. With compass point in x and with radius x–c describe the arc a–c–b. This is the required segment.

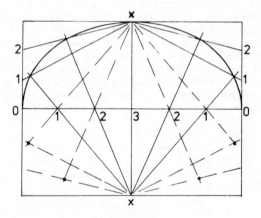

Figure 7.6

Figure 7.6 shows a simple method for constructing an ellipse. Let o–o be the major axis and x–x the minor axis. Draw the rectangle to contain these lines and then divide the major axis into an even number of equal parts. Next, divide each part of the rectangle indicated into the same number of equal parts. Draw lines from the bottom of the minor axis to pass through the points on the major axis to intersect with lines drawn from the top of the minor axis outwards to the points on the rectangle; 1 and 1, 2 and 2, etc. will intersect to give points on the curve of the ellipse. This procedure is called the intersecting lines method.

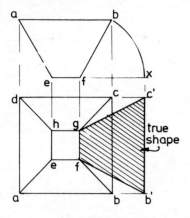

Figure 7.7

Figure 7.7 shows how inclined surfaces can be developed. The drawings may be taken to represent a box with four sloping sides. Let a–b–c–d–e–f–g–h be the plan of the box and a–e–f–b be the elevation. To develop the shape of side b–c–g–f place the compass point in f in the elevation and with radius f–b describe the arc to give x on the horizontal line brought out from f. Drop a vertical line from x to intersect with horizontal lines brought out from c and b in the plan to give points b′ and c′. b′–c′–g–f is the true shape of the side or surface.

8

Marking Out and Setting Out Work

Before most pieces of woodwork can be made it is first necessary to take certain steps so that mistakes can be avoided. This does not apply to all jobs, as has already been implied. The steps referred to are setting out, which means making certain full-size drawings—in the trade this is called making a workshop rod, compiling a list of timber required for the job, and placing the necessary marks on the timber from the information on the rod. Remember, if the rod is incorrect and the errors are not put right, the finished job will also not be correct.

MAKING A WORKSHOP ROD

Let us take two examples. The first (figure 8.1) is the elevation of what is required to be made: it is a simple, single-panelled cupboard

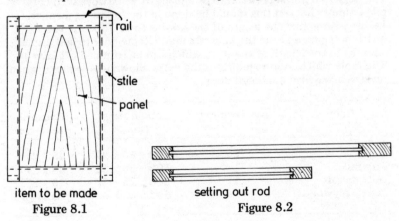

item to be made
Figure 8.1

setting out rod
Figure 8.2

door. Now, this drawing would be of no use as a rod, although many woodworkers would no doubt be able to make the door from this drawing. The drawing does not, however, give all the information required to make the door if mistakes are to be avoided. For instance, the drawing does not indicate the thickness of the door, it does not show the thickness of the panel, and, although it shows that no mouldings are to be placed on the front of the door, no indication is given of the shapes of the section through the framework. Figure 8.2 illustrates how to make a rod for the door and shows that two drawings are required, a full-size vertical section and a full-size horizontal section through the work. The top drawing, the vertical section, shows the length and thickness of the door and the panel. The rectangular rails and their full-size dimensions are given and the depths of the grooves in the rails are also shown.

The bottom drawing, the horizontal section, shows the width of the door and panel as well as other information already illustrated in the vertical section. These two drawings should be carefully drawn, full-size, on a sheet of paper or plywood, remembering to allow for the planing of the timber. If the timber is to be prepared by planing machine, 5 mm on the width and thickness of each piece should be allowed for planing. For instance, if the stiles and top rail are to be prepared from 50 × 32 mm timber, these would finish 45 × 27 mm after being planed up on the machine. If the timber is to be prepared by hand much less would have to be allowed—say 3 mm on the width and thickness.

TIMBER LISTS

The next step in the production of a piece of woodwork is to compile a timber list and this should be done in the following manner. Let us assume that the length of the door is to be 750 mm, the width 500 mm, and the thickness 32 mm. (Remember to add a small amount to the length of the stiles which can be trimmed off later.) The table which follows indicates the extra allowances required when making a panelled cupboard door.

Item	No. required	Sawn sizes (mm)	Finished sizes (mm)
Stiles	2	780 × 50 × 32	45 × 27
Top rail	1	505 × 50 × 32	45 × 27
Bottom rail	1	505 × 75 × 32	70 × 27
Panel (plywood)	1	655 × 430 × 6	As sawn size

MARKING THE TIMBER

When the timber has been prepared the marking out of each piece
must be completed. First of all, face side and face edge marks should
be placed on the pieces to ensure that no mistakes will be made in
the marking out. (The stiles have to be marked out as a pair, one
left-hand and one right-hand, and if face and edge marks are not on
the timbers when this is being done the result may be two left-hand
or two right-hand stiles.) Figure 8.3 shows how the workshop rod is

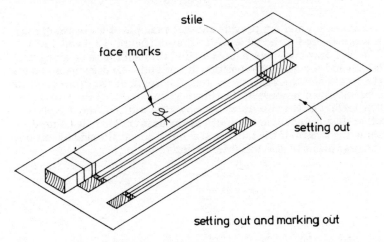

Figure 8.3

used to ensure that the marking out is done correctly. It shows a
stile laid on the setting out so that the appropriate marks can be
made on it. The next step is to place the two stiles together so that
one of the face marks is facing the marker out and the other face
mark on the surface is farthest away from the marker out. This will
ensure that the stiles will be a pair. The rails can also be marked out
in a similar manner, using, of course, the other drawing on the rod.

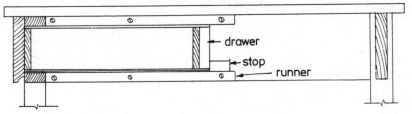

Figure 8.4

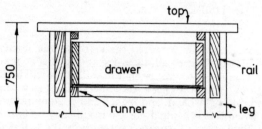

Figure 8.5

Figures 8.4 and 8.5 provide another example of a workshop rod, this one being for the table with a drawer (figures 19.6 and 19.7). The first drawing shows a cross-section through the table along its length and the drawer in position at one end. The drawing also gives the length and thickness of the top, the length of the drawer and the runners which support it, the thickness and depth of the end rail, etc. The second of the two drawings shows the width of the top plus other details including the width of the drawer. There is no need to show the length of the table legs; a dimension at the side of one of the drawings will give this information to the maker.

9

Portable Electric Tools

As with hand tools, it is impossible in writing to teach a person how to use a portable electric tool efficiently. Hand tools are usually much more acceptable than electric tools because most of us have at some time handled many of the various kinds. It is therefore considered prudent to spend a little time in explaining one or two things about portable tools since the teacher in a workshop may be unable to find the time.

With electric tools the potential danger is great, so it is the object of this chapter to give the reader some knowledge of the electric tools he may have available for his use at an evening institute, or, if he can afford them, at home. In addition, some guidance is given on those of the tools available which would most suit his needs.

First of all, the reader must realise that all portable tools are dangerous, so they should be packed away after use to stop children meddling with them and possibly causing injury. The following are some of the rules to be observed when using portable tools.

(1) A person using a portable tool must understand the correct way to use it.
(2) He must know what type of work the tool is capable of doing.
(3) The tool must be kept in good working order and if a fault develops during its use it should be disconnected from the mains and the person responsible for the tool informed. If the tool is for home use it should be taken to a reputable electrician for inspection and repair.
(4) Cables to the tools should be prevented from kinking—since this will lead to breaks—and inspected regularly. They should be replaced by an electrician if damaged.
(5) Tools should not be disconnected from the mains by tugging at the cable. They should not be carried by the cable. This misuse may disconnect the wires from their terminals.
(6) Always take the plug out from the socket when adjusting a portable tool.

(7) Check that the starter switch is in the 'off' position before re-connecting the tool to the mains supply.

(8) Never fix the starter switch in the 'on' position.

(9) If the tool produces dust or abrasive particles, wear goggles and a mask.

(10) Never use a tool without the guards, which have been supplied with the machine, in position.

(11) Where possible, clamp the work down on a bench or on stools before starting the work.

(12) Pay attention to the work you are doing. Don't let anything or anyone distract you.

(13) Let the machine stop before you put it down.

(14) Keep the cable of the tool (or any other tool) away from the cutting edges.

(15) Wear protective clothing if possible.

From this list, which is merely a brief summary of guidelines for the safe use of portable electric tools, it can be seen that common sense plays a large part in safety.

Many education centres are now purchasing double-insulated tools, and, without going into the technicalities of these, it is sufficient to say that they are very safe to use and do not need to be earthed. It is therefore advisable for the reader, if he intends to buy portable tools for home use, to enquire whether the tool that he wants is available double-insulated. Those tools which are not double-insulated must be earthed; this will make it necessary to connect the cable of the machine to a three-pin, 13-amp plug.

The end of the cable furthest from the tool will be seen to have three separate wires, each of which is covered with a different coloured plastics sheathing. It may be necessary for the reader at some time to connect a portable tool to a three-pin plug so he should know the correct way to do this. The 'earth' is the largest of the three pins and is that which is furthest from the point where the cable enters the plug. To this pin is connected the earth wire, colour-ed green and yellow. The other two pins, both situated below the earth pin, are the 'live' and 'neutral'. The brown wire must be con-nected to the live pin (note also that a fuse is incorporated in the wiring adjacent to the live pin), and the wire coloured blue must be connected to the neutral pin. When connecting a two-core cable (that from a double-insulated tool has two wires), ignore the earth pin and connect the brown and the blue cables to the live and neutral terminals, as explained above.

Never insert bare wires into a socket; always fit, or have fitted, the correct type of plug to the tool.

Some readers may be fortunate enough to attend a centre which has a fairly comprehensive range of portable tools. This will cut down, to a large extent, the hard work involved in producing a piece of woodwork.

CIRCULAR SAWS

Perhaps the first tool that should be illustrated—although it is by no means the one which is most used—is the circular saw. The one shown in figure 9.1 is made by Stanley Ltd, but other manufacturers, such as Wolf Ltd and Black and Decker Ltd, also make a wide range of very good electric tools.

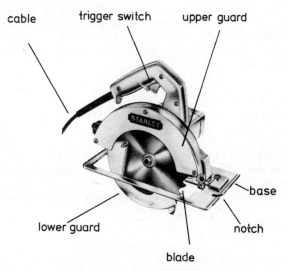

Figure 9.1   Stanley circular saw

Figure 9.2

The most important safety device on all portable circular saws is the lower guard. This guard is spring-loaded and covers the exposed part of the saw blade. When the cut is made the leading end of the timber being cut will push the spring-loaded guard back, as shown in figure 9.2, allowing the cut to be made. When the cut has been completed the guard will spring back into its original position covering the exposed part of the saw again. *Never* fix the guard back.

The machine has a trigger switch for starting and stopping it and the base should rest on the timber when making the cut; a notch in the front edge of the base will enable the operator to cut to a straight line on the timber. The base plate can be adjusted to an angle of 45° to allow bevelled cuts to be made. The saw should be allowed to reach top speed before it is brought in contact with the timber. Do not force the saw.

SABRE SAWS

Figure 9.3 shows a Stanley sabre saw, or, as this type is sometimes called, a jig saw. This is a very useful tool for cutting curved lines. Some models will operate at different speeds. As with the circular saw, bevelled cuts can be made by adjustment of the sole plate.

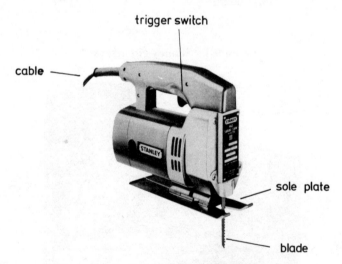

trigger switch

cable

sole plate

blade

Figure 9.3 Stanley sabre saw

DRILLS

Drills are possibly the most used of the portable tools. They can be purchased as single-speed, two-speed, four-speed and percussion tools. The cutting of holes in different materials requires different speeds; for instance, drilling a hole in concrete requires a much slower rotating speed than does the drilling of a hole in a piece of timber. Percussion drills, which have both a rotating action and a hammering effect, are ideal for drilling holes in materials such as concrete.

Figure 9.4b shows a Stanley portable drill and figure 9.4a shows the drill secured in a drilling stand. The stand should be fixed to a bench and with the timber placed on the metal table of the stand the drill can be lowered on to the wood by the lever labelled in the illustration.

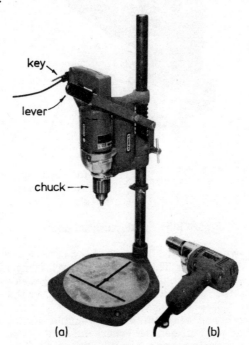

Figure 9.4 Stanley drill and stand

Morse drills are the type to use in a portable drill and these can be fitted into the chuck by using a key which fits into a steadying hole in the chuck side, the teeth on the key fitting into the corresponding teeth on the chuck. To avoid losing the key clip it on the cable when not in use.

SANDING MACHINES

The orbital sander shown in figure 9.5 is one of three common types of portable sanding machine in use today and is the type most suitable for the finishing of joinery work. It is the Stanley orbital sander, which has two speeds of 5500 and 3800 orbitals per minute. It can sand into corners quite easily.

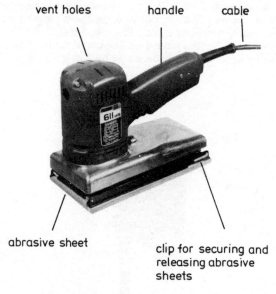

Figure 9.5 Stanley orbital sander

The trigger switch, situated below the handle, has a locking pin to lock it in the 'on' position. This is a particularly safe machine to use, so the locking of the switch does not raise the danger element a great deal. To release the switch all one has to do is depress the switch again.

Sanding sheets soon wear out and it is a simple task to replace them with new ones. Different tools have different devices to do this but they are all very simple and take very little time. The one shown in figure 9.5 has a clip at each end that has to be raised to allow the release of the old sheet and the insertion of the new one. One end should be secured with the new sheet inserted before attempting to insert the sheet in the other end. To use the tool hold the machine firmly and switch on. Apply to the working surface and, using light pressure, guide the machine over the surface until the required finish is obtained. Keep the sander moving all the time.

PLANING MACHINE

Figure 9.6 shows a Wolf electric planer. This is a most useful tool if a lot of planing has to be done and no fixed machine is available. It is used in exactly the same way as a metal jack plane but care must of course be taken because it is a much heavier instrument.

Figure 9.6

The tool illustrated has a 136 mm width of cut and can make cuts 3 mm in depth. It has two cutters in a circular block which revolves at 16 000 rpm. The depth of cut is adjusted by turning the front handle. The graduations visible in the illustration are in tenths of a millimetre.

Begin by placing the front of the tool on the edge of the timber. Push downwards with the front handle, switch on, and push forwards with the rear handle. As the planing stroke comes to the end, hold the front handle lightly and push downwards on the back handle. For a good class finish, have a shallow depth of cut and push the machine over the timber at medium speed.

ROUTERS

The electric router is a most versatile machine and is capable of performing a wide range of operations such as moulding, rebating,

grooving, etc. It must be treated with respect since it can prove to
be highly dangerous. Figure 9.7 shows a Stanley router being used
for trimming the edge of some plastics laminate.

Figure 9.7

Most routers have shaft locking devices which are used when
releasing and inserting cutters in the chuck. Since most manufacturers
have their own particular devices for these tools, it is necessary to
refer to their instructions before attempting to insert cutters and to
adjust them to give the required depth of cut. Having set up the
machine, its base should be placed on the timber, the machine started and allowed to reach maximum speed and then fed on to the
timber. Keep the tool moving or burning of the timber will take
place at the point of pause.

ABRASIVE WHEELS

Most people, at some time or another, use a grinding machine (figure
9.8). This is termed a bench grinder because it can be secured to a
bench. Abrasive wheels must be maintained correctly since they are
potentially very dangerous. Among the many safety hints which

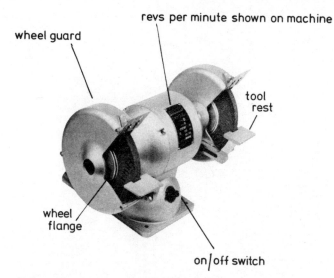

wheel guard

revs per minute shown on machine

tool rest

wheel flange

on/off switch

Note: where no eye protection is fitted goggles must be worn.

Figure 9.8   Stanley bench grinder

should be fully understood by those who are responsible for the machine and those who will be using it are the following.

(1) Always store and handle the wheels with care.
(2) Inspect each wheel visually before mounting it in the machine.
(3) Inspect the label on the wheel to ensure that the speed of the machine suits the maximum permissible speed of the wheel.
(4) Make sure that the work rest is properly adjusted. This should be no more than 3 mm from the wheel and it should either be level with its centre or be slightly above.
(5) Guard as much of the wheel as possible.
(6) Always wear goggles or some other form of eye protection when grinding.
(7) Never use a wheel which has been dropped. It may disintegrate during use.
(8) Never exceed the maximum operating speed of the wheel.
(9) Never grind on the side of a wheel.
(10) Never jam a piece of work on to a wheel.
(11) Never stand in front of a wheel when it is first started.
(12) Never grind a material for which the wheel is not intended.

Part II

Projects

10

Mould Boxes for Concrete

Concrete can play an important part in improving the appearance of a garden. Paving slabs—of various colours if required—and concrete bricks for walls, etc., are only two items which the householder can manufacture himself at a small cost compared with what he would have to pay if he purchased his goods from a concrete products firm.

Mould boxes for the concrete are fairly easy to produce; no complicated joints are required and simplicity in the construction of the boxes is commonplace rather than the exception.

Concrete is manufactured from shingle, sand and cement. The first two can be purchased separately or already mixed, in which case it is called ballast. There are different 'mixes' for various items; for instance, the first item to be discussed, the paving slabs, would need a fairly strong mix, 3:3:2, which means three parts shingle, three parts sand and two parts cement. At this point it should be noted that the best sand to purchase for this type of work is sharp sand—building sand is more suitable for mortar when building brickwork. If ballast has been purchased instead of shingle and sharp sand, the mix for the slabs should be 3:1 (three parts ballast to one part cement). This will also be a fairly strong mix, too strong for the concrete bricks for a wall. These would require a mix of 4:2:1—four of shingle, two of sand and one of cement—or, if ballast were purchased, 6:1, six of ballast and one of cement.

MOULD BOX FOR PAVING SLABS

Figure 10.1 shows how simple it is to produce paving slabs. Four pieces of timber, 38 × 38 mm or 50 × 50 mm, depending on the thickness of slab required, should be jointed together as shown to produce the slabs to the required sizes. One method used to keep the timbers together until the concrete has hardened is shown: a bolt at each end that can easily be undone to release the timbers. If bolts are not available the method shown in figure 10.2 can be used. This involves

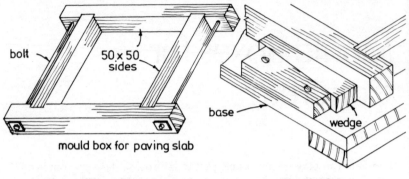

bolt

50 x 50 sides

base

wedge

mould box for paving slab

Figure 10.1   Figure 10.2

having a base board on to which the timber can be placed. Pairs of folding wedges should be made, one member of each pair being screwed to the base board so that when the second one is positioned it will hold the side of the box in place.

MOULD BOX FOR CONCRETE BRICKS

Figure 10.3 shows a mould box for producing ten concrete bricks at a time. The box consists of two sides of fairly large timber (say 50 mm thick), which are recessed to receive the ends of the 19 mm divisions. The sizes of the bricks can vary according to requirements; a common size is 225×100 mm $\times 75$ mm.

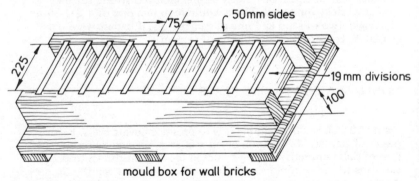

75

50mm sides

225

19 mm divisions

100

mould box for wall bricks

Figure 10.3

In all cases, it is much better to purchase prepared timber for mould boxes since a much cleaner product will be made. Concrete tends to stick to the timber so, to prevent damage when striking (dismantling) the box, it is usual to paint the inner surfaces with a vegetable oil called mould oil.

CONCRETE SPUR BOX

Wooden fence posts have a tendency to rot just below ground level and one method for repairing the fence is to insert a concrete spur in the ground just behind each post and bolt the two together. A mould box for fence spurs is shown in figure 10.4a. Each spur should be about 1 m in length and 100 × 100 mm at the base. Two holes in the concrete will allow the spur to be bolted to the wooden post. The holes can be made by placing two pieces of 12 mm mild steel (m.s.) rod through holes in the box and removing them about an hour after the concrete has been placed in position.

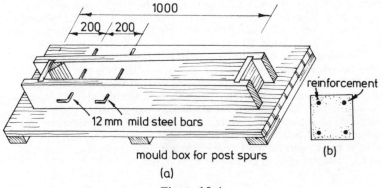

mould box for post spurs

(a)

(b)

Figure 10.4

A triangular piece of timber placed loosely at the top end of the box will give a 'weathering' to the spur. Spurs should be reinforced with metal rod so fairly heavy galvanised-wire lengths should be placed in the box during filling, making sure one piece of wire is near to each of the four corners of the spur (see figure 10.4b). The concrete should be mixed in the proportions 4:2:1.

MAKING CONCRETE LINTELS

Figure 10.5 shows the position of a concrete lintel over an opening in a wall (such as a window opening). Small additions to the home

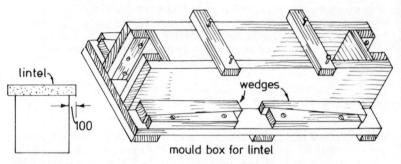

Figure 10.5   Figure 10.6

will sometimes necessitate making one or more lintels and figure 10.6 shows how to make a mould box to produce these. A base board is required on to which the four pieces of timber which will form the box can be placed. The longer sides have battens nailed or screwed to them against which the ends of the box can be placed thus avoiding having to recess the sides to receive the ends. The box should be made from 25 mm timbers to the sizes required. The lintel, when in position on the wall, should have a seating of approximately 100 mm at each end (see figure 10.5).

The sides of the box can be held in position with wedges on the base board, and distance pieces nailed across the top edges of the box. Leave the heads of the nails protruding so that they can easily be removed with a claw hammer. The concrete mix should be the same as for the post spurs. When filling the box remember to place in position, about 25 mm from the base board, a 12 mm diameter m.s. reinforcement rod. This is necessary when a concrete beam such as a lintel has to carry a load; one rod is required for every 100 mm of width. The rod should be shaped as in figure 10.7.

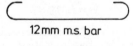

12 mm m.s. bar

Figure 10.7

11
Ladders

STEP-LADDERS

Ladders are essential items for all house owners and there are two types which should be of special interest to the home woodworker, that which is used for work inside the house and that which is more suitable for outside jobs. Figures 11.1a and b show a side and a front view of a step-ladder. They represent the ladder in the open position. The timber necessary for this work is two stringers, which can be made from 100 × 25 mm material, the steps, from 125 × 25 mm timbers, the framed stay, which can be constructed from 100 × 25 mm and 50 × 25 mm timbers, and the top rest and rear batten, from 150 × 25 mm timbers.

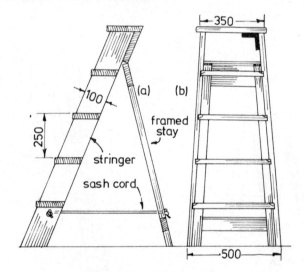

Figure 11.1

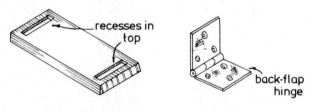

Figure 11.2   Figure 11.3

The width of the steps should be about 500 mm across the lower end, tapering to approximately 350 mm at the top. The steps are recessed about 6 mm into the stringers and are then glued and nailed into position. The top rest is recessed to receive the top ends of the stringers (figure 11.2) and these are connected in the same way. The batten at the rear, to which the framed stay is hinged, is glued and screwed to the stringers. The framed stay is morticed and tenoned together, the joints being glued and wedged. The stay should be hinged to the steps with back-flap hinges (figures 11.3 and 11.4) and the front top corners of the steps should be removed with chisel and mallet as shown in figure 11.5.

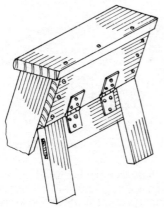

Figure 11.4   Figure 11.5

LADDERS FOR OUTSIDE WORK

For outside work a ladder similar to that shown in figure 11.6 is desirable. It consists of two stringers and a number of crosspieces called rungs. The best way to make such a ladder is to mortice and tenon the rungs to the stringers, securing the joints with a good synthetic resin glue and wedges. When the ladder has been assembled, 6 mm diameter wire ties should be placed immediately beneath the top, bottom and centre rungs and riveted, with a washer beneath the rivet heads (see figure 11.7).

Another method for constructing a ladder for home use is illustrated in figure 11.8. In this method the stringers, which should be prepared from 75 × 50 mm material, are recessed to a depth of, say, 8 mm, to receive the rungs, which are glued and screwed into position.

In the types of ladder shown in figures 11.6 and 11.8, the distance between the rungs should not be more than 250 mm. Care must be

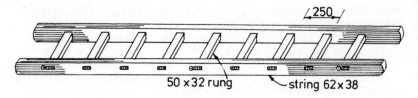

Figure 11.6

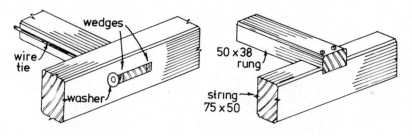

Figure 11.7   **Figure 11.8**

taken when selecting timber for these ladders; it should be straight-grained and free from defects such as knots and splits. The timbers most suitable are Douglas fir, Sitka spruce, European redwood and European whitewood. If the stringers are made from a timber selected from the above list that is straight-grained and free from defects, and if oak rungs are used, then the result should be a good, serviceable ladder.

Do not paint a ladder because this will tend to conceal defects. In addition, if possible, tie the top of the ladder during use, to prevent it from moving in high winds. For safety the top of the ladder should extend at least 1 m beyond the working point. Inspect the ladder regularly, repair as soon as defects begin to show, and return to the garage or other place of store as soon as possible after the work has been completed.

12

Cold Frames

Cold frames are an asset in any garden. Figure 12.1 shows a cold
frame which is very simple to make. The sides of the frame are made
from 9 mm external grade plywood, tapering from, say, 300 mm at
the back to approximately 150 mm at the front. The length and
width dimensions can be around 1 m by 1.5 m, but of course these,
as well as the height measurements, can be varied to suit personal
requirements. The sides of the box can be secured by gluing and
screwing to 50 × 50 mm pieces of timber, and the top edges of the
sides can be stiffened with 50 × 25 mm pieces, also glued and
screwed into position.

The ground should be prepared by placing a 150 × 100 mm
concrete base strip just below the surface of the ground, as shown
in figure 12.2. To make sure the concrete is level all round, pegs
should be driven in the bottom of the trench and levelled in the way
illustrated in figure 12.3.

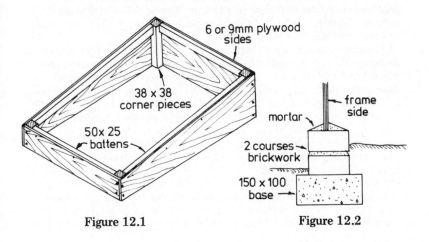

Figure 12.1

Figure 12.2

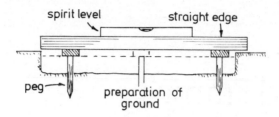

Figure 12.3

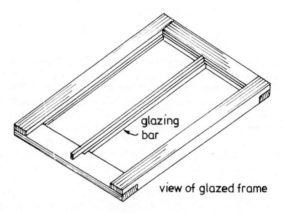

view of glazed frame

Figure 12.4

When the concrete has set, two courses (at least) of brickwork should be laid around the concrete base so that the frame can be positioned on top well clear of the soil. A good fillet of mortar should be placed on top of the brickwork (figure 12.2) to throw off the water which may settle there.

The glazed frame which will be placed on top of the box is shown in figure 12.4. It consists of a top and a bottom rail, two stiles (side pieces) and a glazing bar. The stiles and top rail should be made from, say, 100 × 38 mm timber, the bottom rail from 100 × 25 mm, and the glazing bar from 38 × 38 mm. In a case such as this the jointing of the pieces should be carried out by as simple a method as possible. It is suggested that halving joints should be used. These are shown in figures 12.5a, b and c. At (a) is seen one end of the top rail. The depth of the portion removed is equal to the depth of the glass rebate. The small mortice towards the left is to receive the tenon on the top end of the glazing bar. At (b) is seen one end of the bottom rail. Since the bottom rail is equal in thickness to the other pieces, less the depth of the rebates, nothing has to be done to its ends. The recess towards the left of this piece is to receive the lower end of the

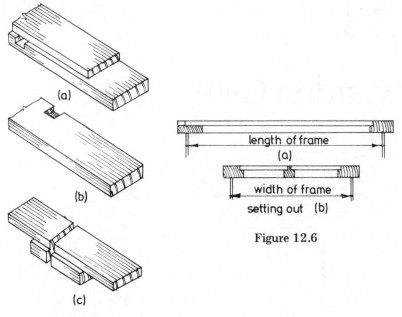

length of frame
(a)

width of frame

setting out (b)

Figure 12.6

(a)

(b)

(c)

Figure 12.5

glazing bar. At (c) is shown a shortened view of one of the stiles. In
this case the portion below the rebate at each end is removed.

Figures 12.6a and b show how to set out a rod for the glazed
frame. Draw the over-all dimensions of the box first so as to ensure
that the glazed frame will be made to the correct sizes, bearing in
mind also that the glazed frame should overlap the box by something
like 50 mm. After making the cold frame the timbers should be given
a liberal coating of preservative—not creosote, but one which will not
damage plant life.

13

Garden Gate

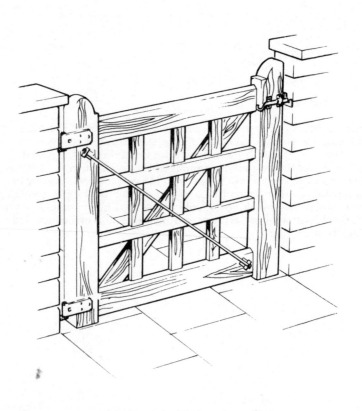

The first object a visitor to a house sees may well be the entrance gate to the property. So why not an attractive gate? Of course, what is attractive to one person may not be attractive to another, so the designer is really pleasing himself in the first instance and hoping that his taste is not far removed from that of the average person. The entrance gate shown in figure 13.1 can be made from a softwood such as red or yellow deal and should be painted, first with a good quality pink priming, then with one or two coats of good quality undercoating and finally with a good finishing coat.

Alternatively, the gate can be made from a hardwood such as oak, teak, etc. Hardwoods should not be painted but should be allowed to show off their natural beauty; two or three coats of external varnish or clear polyurethane will allow this.

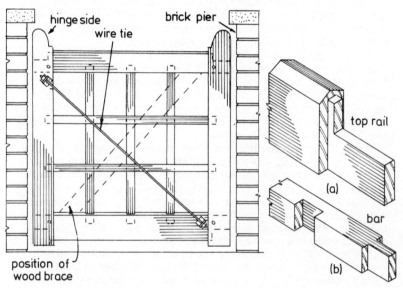

Figure 13.1   Figure 13.2

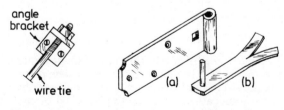

Figure 13.3   Figure 13.4

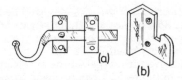

Figure 13.5

The timber sizes for a gate such as the one shown should be : top rail and stiles from 100 × 50 mm, bottom rail from 125 × 50 mm and the bars from 32 × 32 mm material. Of course, these measurements are only a guide and can be adjusted as necessary.

The stiles have been allowed to extend upwards beyond the top rail so that they can be shaped. The top edges of the top and bottom rails have been bevelled from the centre to throw off any water which may tend to collect there (see figure 13.2a).

The four main pieces of timber have been jointed with haunched mortice and tenon joints and then glued with a synthetic resin and pinned (12 mm dowels should be used). The bars are halved at their intersections and stub-morticed and tenoned to the frame timbers. Remember to make bevelled shoulders on the three vertical bars where they intersect with the bottom rail. The joints for the gate are shown in figures 13.2a and b.

It can be argued that braces are not required in many of the jobs which required them when animal glues were used in joinery. With modern glues many people say that braces are not required because joints are so strong that there is little chance of the glue's breaking up. There is, of course, a lot in this argument, so braces are probably not required in gate construction. However, to be on the safe side, a brace has been included in the gate shown in figure 13.1 This is not a timber brace but one made from a stout wire or 6 mm mild steel rod. Wire is strong in tension so the brace must be positioned with its top end near to the hinge side of the gate. If a timber brace (also shown in figure 13.1) were to be used, its lower end would be nearer to the hinge side of the gate. The wire brace should be threaded at each end and secured to small angle brackets (see figure 13.3).

GATE HINGES

If the gate is to be hinged to a brick pier the type of hinge required would be similar to that shown in figures 13.4a and b. The part which contains the pin (b) has to be secured to the brickwork by raking out the mortar joints at the appropriate places and cementing the pins in position. The strap hinges should then be screwed to the gate opposite the pin positions. If the pins are to be fixed to a wooden post the pin shown at (c) should be used.

To secure the gate in the closed position the fittings shown in figures 13.5a and b should be purchased. The latch is secured to the gate and the lip, which, incidentally, incorporates a stop, is secured to the brickwork or wooden post. When setting out the rod for the gate be sure to make its width quite a considerable amount less than the distance between the posts or piers. Remember, too, that if oak is used it is necessary to prevent the acid contained in the oak from corroding the fittings secured to the gate. These should be well painted before fixing to the woodwork and some polythene can be placed behind each metal part before fixing. The screws used should be galvanised or treated in some other way to prevent rusting.

14

Shelving

There are various forms of shelving and the type selected usually depends on where it is to be fixed and for what purpose it is intended.

Figure 14.1 shows a common method for supporting a shelf which fits into a recess. Battens should be prepared and plugged and ·screwed to the wall at each end. The battens can be of any size—around 50 × 25 mm or 38 × 19 mm are common sizes—and their lengths should be slightly less than the width of the shelf. The shelf in this case is a piece of blockboard with a lipping along its front edge.

Timber, being the expensive material it is, can be replaced with a built-up shelf similar to that shown in figure 14.2. This consists of two strips of timber, say 38 × 19 mm, with 3 mm plywood or tempered hardboard glued and pinned to form the two surfaces of the shelf. A lipping can then be glued and pinned along its front edge as in the previous example.

If a shelf is to be fixed to a wall and is not in a recess, metal brackets similar to that illustrated in figure 14.3 should be purchased. This is not a method to be recommended where the look of the shelf is important because it is by no means attractive. This type of shelf and its supports are more suitable for use in a garage, larder or store.

The correct method for fixing metal brackets of the kind shown in figure 14.3 is first to plug a batten on the wall and then to screw the bracket to the batten. If the bracket is fixed directly to the wall the screw holes in the bracket will have to be enlarged so that screws of a suitable size can be used.

The centre of a bookshelf can be supported unobtrusively by using a metal bracket similar to that shown in figure 14.4. The bracket is fixed on top of the shelf and plugged to the wall. It will not be seen because it will be hidden by the books.

Of much better quality, and suitable for a lounge or any other living area in the house, are the shelf and supports illustrated in figures 14.5 and 14.6. The supports are non-ferrous metal angle and

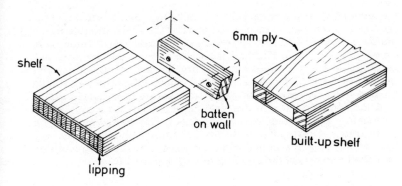

Figure 14.1

Figure 14.2

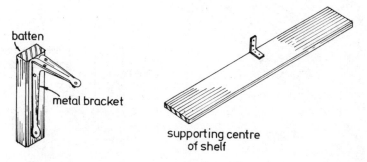

Figure 14.3

Figure 14.4

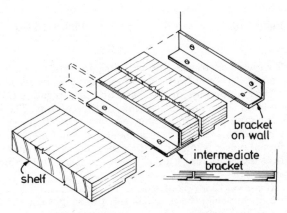

Figure 14.5

Figure 14.6

tee sections. The angle brackets, assuming the shelf fits in a recess, are fixed to the wall to receive the ends of the shelf. Intermediate brackets should be of the tee section variety and one of these is also shown in figure 14.5. This bracket has to be built into the wall and naturally neatness is important. The bracket section should pass into the wall at least 75 mm, and the metal which enters the wall should be bent slight by striking with a hammer before it is passed into the wall and cemented in. The brackets should be left for a couple of days before any loading is placed on them. The shelf, which should be a hardwood matching the décor of the room, should be cut carefully to the lengths required and each piece should be shaped to fit over the brackets, as shown in figures 14.5 and 14.6.

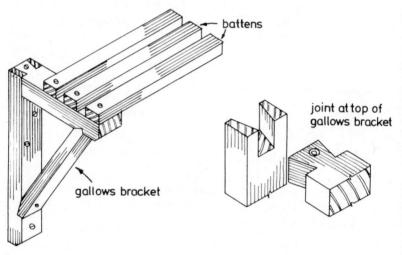

Figure 14.7   Figure 14.8

Figure 14.7 shows a shelf, together with its supports, which is suitable for use in a garage or outhouse where heavy loads are likely to be carried. The supports are in the shape of wooden gallows brackets, made from timber of 50 × 38 mm or thereabouts. The vertical and horizontal pieces are connected by a dovetailed joint (see figure 14.8) and this should be glued and screwed together. The brace, the diagonal piece, is joined to the other pieces by simple recessed joints as drawn in figure 14.7. These are glued and screwed into position.

The shelf can consist of strips of wood, say 50 × 32 mm (depending on the distance between the brackets and the weight the shelf has to carry) and these strips should be evenly spaced across the supports and screwed into position.

Shelves are used for a variety of purposes and it is often necessary to change the height of a shelf. For instance, bookshelves may be used for smaller sizes of books at one time and at another they may be required to support larger ones. If these situations are foreseen it is as well to install shelves with adjustable heights. Figure 14.9 provides details of how this can be carried out. Two notched battens secured vertically at each end of the cabinet or bookcase, as shown in figure 14.9, are made to receive a batten or shelf-rest and are all that is required. The shelf-rest must be bevelled at each end so that it will fit into the ledges of the vertical pieces. In addition, the shelf should be shaped to fit round the notched battens as illustrated in the figure.

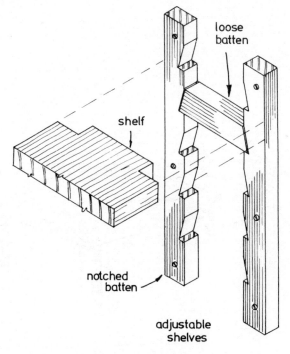

Figure 14.9

Very attractive shelving can be obtained by using wrought iron brackets and melamine-covered chipboard. Remember to include a sufficient number of brackets to prevent chipboard shelves from sagging.

15

Coffee Table

There are many ways of constructing a coffee table, some more difficult than others. It can be made from a hardwood, such as mahogany, teak, oak or another, equally attractive timber, or from a softwood, such as Douglas fir. The timber can be finished with clear polyurethane so that the natural grain will be visible. Alternatively, a good quality softwood such as red or yellow deal, painted according to preference, may be used.

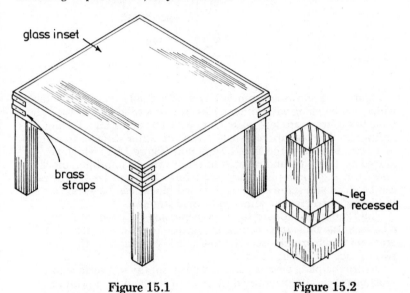

Figure 15.1   **Figure 15.2**

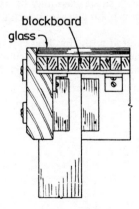   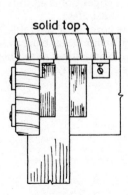

Figure 15.3   **Figure 15.4**

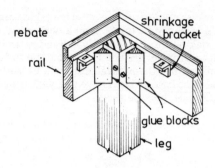

Figure 15.5

Figure 15.1 shows an isometric view of a small square coffee table which can be made with either a glass top or a solid timber top. The table has four square legs made from 50 × 50 mm or 62 × 62 mm hardwood. The legs are recessed on the two outer surfaces to a depth of 10 mm to receive the 75 × 19 mm rails (figure 15.2) which are mitred at their ends and rebated to receive the 12 mm-thick block-board top and 6 mm plate glass (see figures 15.3 and 15.4). The rails can be glued and screwed to the legs and blocks can be glued to the inside angles to give the joints additional strength.

The 12 mm blockboard top is prepared and dropped into the rebates in the rails. It is secured in position by means of shrinkage brackets which are first secured to the inside surfaces of the rails, two to each rail (figure 15.5).

Before the plate glass is placed in position, the top surface of the blockboard should be covered. A piece of leatherette, a print or a map are examples of materials which could be used to fulfil this purpose. The glass should be cut to fit easily in place and finish flush with the tops of the rails. Thirty-two-ounce sheet glass may be used and its edges polished, but naturally, 6 mm plate glass is superior to 32 oz sheet glass.

The corners of the table may be decorated with thin brass straps, say, 150 mm long, bent to form a right angle. These can be drilled to receive some brass raised-headed or round-headed screws, which are fairly easy to buy.

16

Garden Seat

This type of garden furniture should be made from a timber which is resistant to dampness. A timber such as teak, oak or iroko is ideal for the type of outside conditions which prevail in the United Kingdom throughout the year. These timbers, too, are attractive in appearance and all they need to keep them in good repair is an occasional coating of external-grade varnish or polyurethane.

If, however, a softwood timber is used in the manufacture of the seat, the timber should be given a couple of coats of a good preservative such as Cuprinol, which can be painted over. In addition, a softwood seat should be stood on shallow blocks of some sort to keep the legs away from direct contact with the ground. Small blocks of slate, if it is possible to obtain these, would be ideal, otherwise a material such as terra-cotta tiles would suffice.

Figure 16.1 shows a pictorial view of a garden seat made mainly from 50×50 mm or 62×62 mm ($2\frac{1}{2}$ in. $\times 2\frac{1}{2}$ in.) timbers, the latter obviously being preferable. All the timbers except for those which form the seat, are morticed and tenoned together, the joints being dowelled and glued with a synthetic resin glue such as Cascomite.

Figure 16.2 represents a section through the seat; this shows that the dimensions of that part of the structure which is sat upon are 450 mm wide by 400 mm from ground level. These dimensions can be adjusted if required. About 500 mm (20 in.) should be allowed for each person with a maximum of three persons when the seat is fully occupied. Two end frames, the shape of which can be seen in figure 16.2, will be required for the seat. Those pieces of timber, which extend from one end frame to the other, should be prepared from timbers at least 100 mm in depth by 38 mm in thickness. The seating slats, which should be around 50×25 mm in size, rest on the end frames and on a crosspiece at their centres.

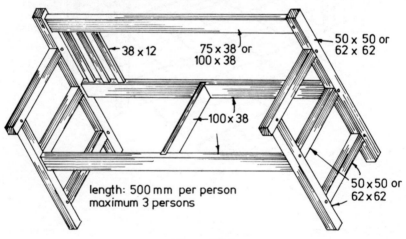

Figure 16.1

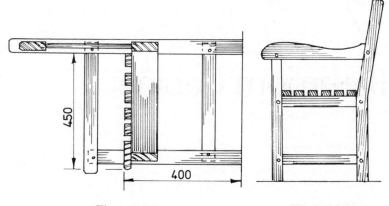

Figure 16.2   Figure 16.3

The back of the seat is completed by using 38 × 12 mm slats spaced at equal intervals.

Figures 16.1 and 16.2 show a very plain type of seat with an upright back. Figure 16.3 is a drawing similar to figure 16.2 but has some refinements. For instance, the back is sloping, which of course means that wider timbers would be required for the rear components of the end frames. In addition, the arm rests have been shaped and rounded on their top edges for extra comfort.

In each of the examples, where possible the timbers should be chamfered to take off their sharp corners, especially around the lower ends of the feet; this will prevent the tendency of the timbers to split when the seat is dragged along the ground.

17

Bathroom Cabinet

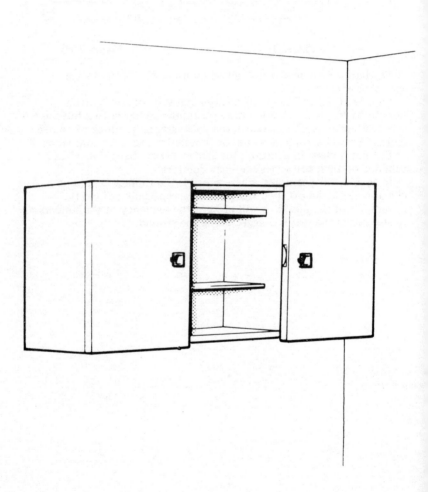

This is a fairly simple object to make (see figure 17.1). The dimensions for the cabinet can be determined according to preference but it would be a mistake to make it too large. Suggested dimensions are 600 mm in length, 350 mm in depth, and 150 mm from front to back. Details of its construction are shown in figure 17.2.

The main part of the cabinet is made from four pieces of timber—12 mm blockboard, if it is to be covered with white laminated plastics, which is suggested—either butt-jointed at the corners or lapped-jointed as shown in the drawing. If the cabinet is to be covered with plastics, it is suggested that butt joints be used; these are glued and nailed together and the plywood back is nailed on to the back edges of the four pieces. If solid timber or blockboard lipped on the front edges, is to be used, the plywood back should be rebated in position (see figure 17.2).

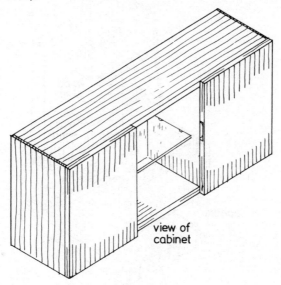

view of cabinet

Figure 17.1

If the method shown in figure 17.3 is used for fixing the cabinet to the wall then it is necessary to fix the plywood back in the way also shown in the figure. This consists of grooving the four pieces of timber which form the main part of the cabinet about 25 mm from their back edges so that the plywood can be assembled into the cabinet while the sides are being secured together. The two pieces forming the inner sides of the two cupboards should be jointed to the top and bottom pieces by fitting them into stopped housings and securing by means of glue and nails. A method for cutting the grooves for the stopped housing joints is shown in figure 17.4. After

marking out the joint a brace and bit should be used for boring two
or three holes to the depth of the groove near to its stopped end.
That portion of the groove can then be chopped out with mallet
and chisel, and the tenon saw can be used for cutting down the sides
of the remaining part of the groove. This will enable the rest of the
groove to be completed with the chisel and mallet.

Shelves in the cupboard sections will no doubt be required, and a
shelf in the exposed part of the cabinet will also be useful. A wooden
or (preferably) a glass shelf can be fitted in this section. The alterna-
tives are shown in figure 17.2.

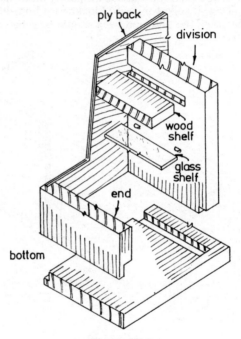

Figure 17.2

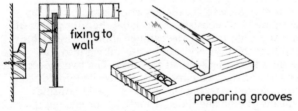

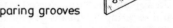

Figure 17.3   **Figure 17.4**   **Figure 17.5**

Plate or sheet glass 6 mm thick, its edges polished to avoid sharp corners, should be used if a glass shelf is preferred. With patience the reader can polish his piece of glass with medium-coarse oilstone, by holding it at 45° to the corners of the glass and rubbing them away— as when the arris from a piece of wood is removed.

The doors of the cabinet are made from solid wood or block-board—which should of course be lipped if not covered with plastics— and each should be hinged with two 38 mm or 50 mm brass butts and screws. The inside edges of the doors should be recessed for easy opening, as shown in figure 17.1, and magnetic catches should be fitted to keep the doors in the closed position.

The cabinet can be fixed to the bathroom wall with two mirror plates (figure 17.5), or the method shown in figure 17.3 can be used. A lipped batten of 50 × 25 mm timber should be secured to the cup-board just below the top, as shown in the figure, and a similar piece secured to the wall so that the former will fit over the top of the latter. This method will allow the cupboard to be removed and re-fixed with a minimum of trouble.

18
Free-standing Cupboard

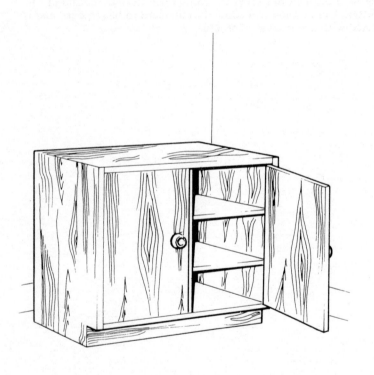

The sizes shown in figure 18.1 for a free-standing cupboard are suggested dimensions, but a height of 900 mm is likely to be more convenient if the top of the cupboard is to be utilised as a working surface in the kitchen.

The cupboard can be made from blockboard 12 or 19 mm thick and covered with a laminated plastics. The skirting at the bottom front edge should be recessed as shown, to allow for toe space.

Figure 18.2 represents a vertical cross-section through the cupboard and shows its construction. The cupboard has two shelves, positioned as required, which rest on battens screwed to the cupboard sides. The shelf rests must not be glued since it may be necessary to move the positions of the shelves at a later date.

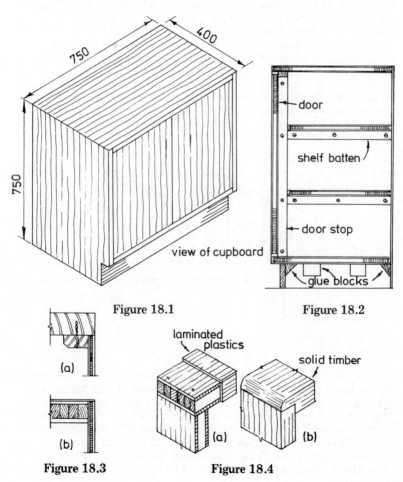

Figure 18.1

Figure 18.2

Figure 18.3

Figure 18.4

All the pieces of blockboard used to construct the cupboard, including the shelves, should be lipped with thin pieces of solid wood. The lippings should be glued and pinned in position. The skirting should be set back to a depth of around 40 mm from the front edge of the cupboard bottom and should be secured with glue and screws. The back of the cupboard, which should be made from 6 mm plywood, can be secured in one of two ways, as shown in figures 18.3a and b. If solid timber is used for constructing the cupboard, method (a) can be employed. Battens are glued and screwed around the top, sides and bottom of the cupboard and are set back from the rear edges of these pieces to a distance equal to the thickness of the plywood back. If the cupboard is to be covered with a laminated plastics, method (b) can be used. The plywood is glued and nailed directly on to the back edges of the top and sides and must be allowed to extend down to floor level (figure 18.2).

Glue blocks should be used for strengthening the cupboard at ...or level. The blocks are obtained from square pieces of timber cut diagonally into two pieces and trimmed to about 75–100 mm in length. Each block should be glued on the two surfaces which form a right angle, then eased into position and tacked to keep it in position until the glue sets. Glue blocks should always be used in positions such as that shown in figure 18.2, because they strengthen the structure quite considerably.

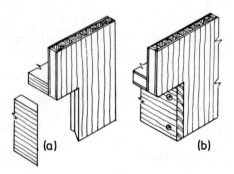

(a) (b)

Figure 18.5

The joints to use between the top and sides may also be influenced by the finish of the cupboard. If it is to be covered with laminated plastics, the butt joint shown in figure 18.4a can be used. Glue and large (50 mm) oval brads will be satisfactory in securing these joints. If solid timber is to be used in the construction of the cupboard the joint at (b) can be used. This is a lapped joint with the corner rounded to give a neat finish. Glue and large panel pins should be used, the heads of the pins being punched below the surface and the depressions filled with a wood filler the colour of which should match that of the wood used.

Figures 18.5a and b show how the recessed skirting can be fitted. At (a) is seen the method to use when the cupboard is constructed from solid timber. The ends of the skirting should be mitred and a joint formed below the bottom of the cupboard to receive the mitred skirting. At (b) is seen the very simple joint required if the woodwork is to be covered with a plastics laminate.

19
Drop-leaf Table

Figure 19.1 represents a pictorial view of a drop-leaf table with provision for a drawer at one end. The legs are square, of, say 50 × 50 mm material, but the more sophisticated, turned, moulded legs can be purchased if desired.

The table is rectangular with two narrow flaps to increase its size when extra width is required. The height of the table should be 750 mm. The length and width are according to personal preference but, to give an idea of convenient sizes, the length of the table could be 1000 mm, the width of the main top 450 mm and of the flaps 150 mm each.

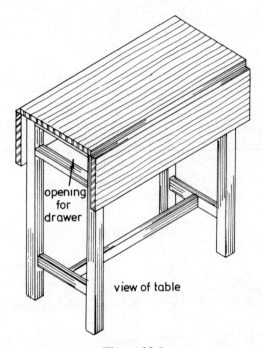

Figure 19.1

Figure 19.2 shows the main points in the construction of the table. The top rails are haunched-morticed and tenoned to the legs. The opening for the drawer is seen to consist of two 50 × 25 mm pieces, the top piece being dovetailed to the legs at each end and the lower piece stub-morticed and tenoned; two tenons are used for this joint. The width of the drawer will be the full width between the two legs so drawer runners will have to be fitted to the rails which run parallel to the drawer. These consist, in each case, of a piece of packing to which the runner is glued and screwed so that the drawer will be supported in position. The joints for the lower rails are also

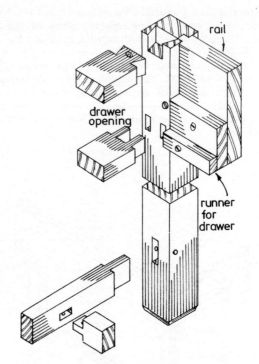

Figure 19.2

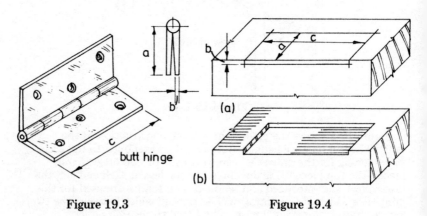

Figure 19.3   **Figure 19.4**

shown in figure 19.2 and should all be glued and dowelled as should all the other mortice and tenon joints in the framing.

The main top of the table should be fixed to the leg framing by means of shrinkage plates as shown in figure 15.5. The flaps can be hinged to the main top with brass hinges and screws (see figures 19.3 and 19.4 for details of fitting), each held in the open position with a pair of brackets (figure 19.5). These can be hinged to the main rail with a brass butt. If difficulty is experienced in securing the screws to the hinge in the end grain of the bracket, back flaps can be used, in which case the hinge would be secured to the side of the bracket and not to its end.

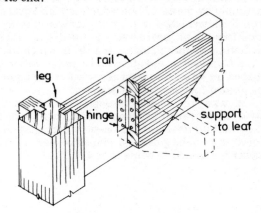

Figure 19.5

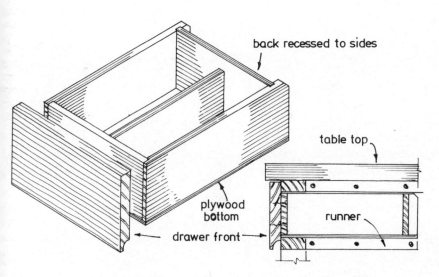

Figure 19.6   Figure 19.7

Incidentally, if difficulty is met in setting out a rod for the table the reader should turn back to chapter 8, where one of the examples taken for setting out is the table under discussion.

Figures 19.6 and 19.7 show a simple way to make a drawer (other examples are explained later). Figure 19.6 shows a pictorial view of the drawer. This consists of a box, the width of which is very slightly less than the width of the opening for the drawer (say, 3 mm), and a front, which is secured to the box later. The box can be made very simply by means of housed joints with a piece of plywood nailed on the lower edges to form the drawer bottom. Divisions for cutlery can be incorporated in the drawer if desired. The front, made from timber to match that from which the table is constructed, can be prepared and glued and screwed to the front of the box. If shaped on its bottom edge as shown in the figure, no handle will be needed for opening the drawer.

Figure 19.7 shows a cross-section through the drawer and its relationship with the surrounding components. To stop the drawer from sliding too far into its recess and possibly damaging the front, a small plywood stop can be glued and pinned on each of the runners where the drawer is required to come to rest.

20
Refectory Table

Another fairly easy piece of essential furniture to make is the refectory table, a view of which is shown in figure 20.1. It consists of a top, of 25 mm solid hardwood or 19 mm lipped blockboard, and two endpieces, legs and rail battens. The table should be 750 mm in height and its length and width are determined according to personal requirements. Figure 20.2 shows an end view of the table and provides an alternative design for the pieces which support the table top.

If lipped blockboard is to be used in the construction of the table top, 19 mm material should be purchased. If this is not considered to be thick enough, the method shown in figure 20.3 should be followed to make the top appear to be much thicker than it actually is. This method can even be adopted where a thinner solid top is required.

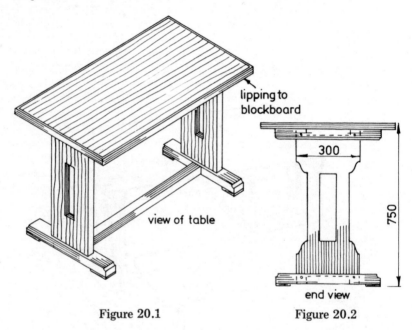

lipping to blockboard

view of table

300

750

end view

Figure 20.1   Figure 20.2

Figure 20.4 shows the types of joint which can be used in making the table. The top supports consist of three pieces of timber: the vertical piece, which should be around 300 mm wide and 38 mm thick, and two lower crosspieces, both obtained from 75 × 50 (or 62) mm material. Each crosspiece is morticed and tenoned to the vertical piece, the joints being glued and dowelled, and should have two pieces of 6 mm plywood (or solid timber) attached to its lower surface to prevent the table from rocking if placed on an unlevel floor.

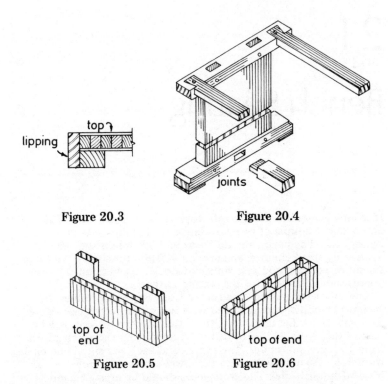

Figure 20.3   **Figure 20.4**

Figure 20.5   **Figure 20.6**

The two bars at the top of the table should be connected to the top supports with dovetailed joints and should be secured with glue and screws. They should be made from 75 × 32 mm timbers. The lower bar, which should be from 75 × 50 (or 62) mm material, is jointed to the vertical supports (see figure 20.4). The joints should be glued and pinned from the bottom.

Figure 20.5 shows the tenon on the top edge of one of the table top supports and figure 20.6 gives an alternative to the tenons. This consists of three 12 mm diameter dowels, the marking out of which should be very carefully carried out. The table top should be secured to the framing by means of six to eight shrinkage plates.

21

Bench Seating

If seating is required for the refectory table (chapter 20), what better than a couple of benches similar to that illustrated in figure 21.1? The height should be around 500 mm if they are to be used by small children and around 400 mm for adults. With considerations of cost and availability of stock sizes in mind, 225 mm boards should be used for the seating surfaces.

The tops need not be constructed from very thick timber, because each bench will be strengthened with two apron pieces (see figures 21.1 and 21.2). Let us assume, then, that the top surfaces will be made either from 25 mm or 32 mm material, and the apron pieces from 75 × 25 mm timber. The supports at each end should be made from 225 × 38 mm timber and the lower crosspieces from 50 × 50 mm material. The crosspieces should be morticed and tenoned to the supports (the joints are represented by the broken line in figure 21.2) and should be secured with glue and dowels. The

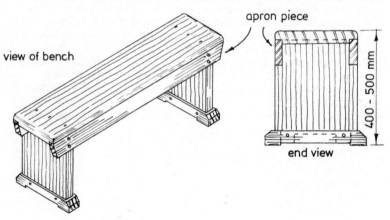

view of bench

apron piece

400 – 500 mm

end view

Figure 21.1

Figure 21.2

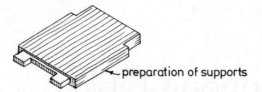
preparation of supports

Figure 21.3

supports are housed in the bottom surfaces of the seat to a depth of about 6 mm and rebates should be made in the lower surface of the seat to accommodate the apron pieces. Recesses should be made in the sides of the supports to receive the apron pieces. The seat boards are glued and nailed to the supports (using 75 mm cut nails if possible), and the apron pieces are attached to them by means of glue and screws.

Rebates into which the apron pieces fit can be made in the seat boards but this is not strictly necessary. However, if this is not done, the recesses in the lower surface of the seat board, which receive the end supports, will have to be stopped, thus making cutting the recesses unnecessarily tedious. Figure 21.3 shows one of the supports ready for assembly.

22
Telephone Table

Figure 22.1 shows an isometric view of a telephone table. The
telephone can be stood on the surface of the section on the left,
which also acts as a useful cupboard for storing such items as note-
pads, pencils and diaries. The right-hand section is used for a seat
and has a space below for housing directories. (Naturally, telephone
users in London will require a larger space for their directories, so
the space below the telephone can be utilised for this purpose and
that under the seat can be put to another use.)

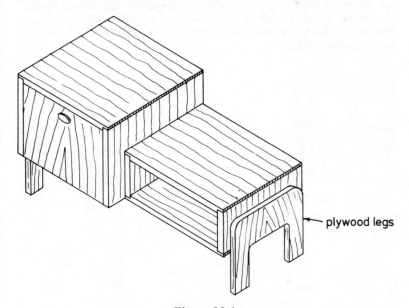

plywood legs

Figure 22.1

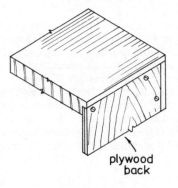

plywood
back

Figure 22.2

The table can be constructed by making the two sections separately, the sizes being adjusted to suit the purpose for which they are to be used, and then screwing them together through the sides that meet. The sections should both be fitted with plywood backs: the method for fitting these is shown in figure 22.2. The fixing of the backs should be left until after the two units have been joined together. The joint at the corners of the two sections may be dowelled (as shown in figure 22.3a) or a recessed joint can be used (see figure 22.3b). To give the table the strength it will require when . it is used as a seat, a fairly substantial piece of timber, say 62 × 50 mm, should be glued and screwed along the bottom surfaces of the two sections (figure 22.3c).

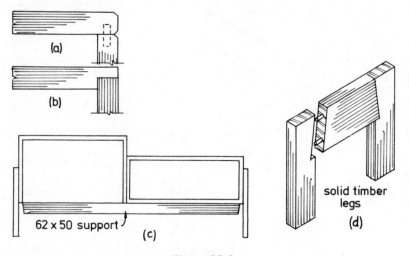

Figure 22.3

The legs of the unit can be made from 12 mm-thick plywood—a simple way of dealing with this problem—or 19 mm solid timber (as shown in figure 22.3d) and are fixed to the ends of the unit with brass raised-headed screws. The legs should extend below the two sections to a distance of approximately 200 mm.

A door may be fitted to one or both units and two brass hinges, fixed to the lower edge, should be used for each door. A small brass quadrant should be fitted to each door so that it will open to a horizontal position rather than hang downwards unsupported on opening. A cupboard doorknob and a magnetic catch complete the work.

23

Bed Head with Drawer Units

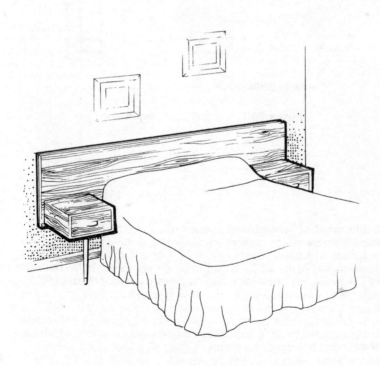

Figure 23.1 shows a view of a bed head with a drawer unit on either side, and figure 23.2 represents a vertical section through the work. The length of the bed head panel should be sufficient to allow the bed to fit between the drawer units and its depth should allow the tops of the latter to lie approximately 100 mm above the top of the mattress.

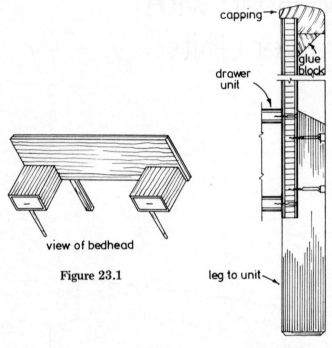

view of bedhead

Figure 23.1

capping

glue block

drawer unit

leg to unit

Figure 23.2

The panel of the bed head consists of a piece of 12 mm veneer-faced blockboard, the veneer on the face matching the décor of the bedroom. The panel should have a 50 × 38 mm moulded capping (as illustrated in figure 23.2). Glue blocks should be placed in the angle made by the panel and cappings as shown, to give additional strength. Two legs, each constructed from 50 × 32 mm timber, should be positioned across the width of the panel and attached from the back with screws.

Details of the drawer units at each end of the panel are illustrated in figures 23.3 to 23.5. Suggested over-all sizes are given, which can be adjusted if desired. Each unit consists of a four-sided box of 15 mm solid wood or 12 mm veneered blockboard. If the former material is used, lapped joints glued and pinned together, with the corners rounded if required, should be used. If the latter is used, butt

joints, glued and pinned, should be used. The ends and the front
edges of the boards that show the bare wood should be covered with
strips of matching veneer, and the pin holes should be filled with a
matching wood filler.

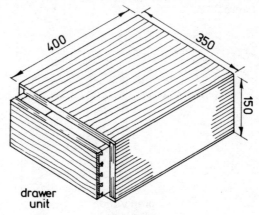

Figure 23.3

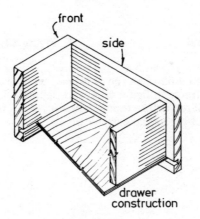

Figure 23.4

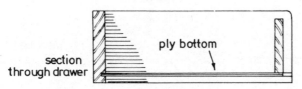

Figure 23.5

The drawer details are shown in figures 23.4 and 23.5. The sides are dovetailed to the front and the back is recessed into the sides using stopped housings. Both front and sides are grooved to receive the 3 mm (or 6 mm) plywood bottoms. The boxes containing the drawers are secured to the bed head panel by means of screws, as indicated in figure 23.2.

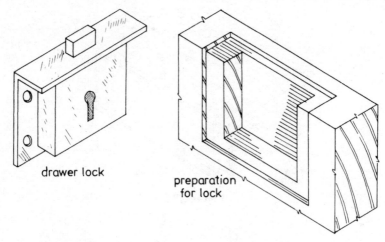

drawer lock

preparation for lock

Figure 23.6   Figure 23.7

Locks may be required on the drawers. The type of lock to purchase is illustrated in figure 23.6, and figure 23.7 shows the preparation required before fixing. It is also, of course, necessary to mark out and cut the keyhole with care.

24

Wall-Units

Wall units (figure 24.1) are currently fashionable. They are very simple to make and with care and precision in their preparation they can be a very attractive and useful addition to the home. Many of the units purchased from stores are made from melamine-covered chipboard and since it is easy to obtain the home woodworker will find this material useful when making objects such as wall units and shelving.

The joints used by manufacturers are simple to produce by means of machinery but are not so simple for the amateur woodworker to make by hand in his own home or in the workshop of an evening institute. If solid wood is to be used to make a wall unit the task of producing woodworking joints at the intersections of its many components is simple. Lapped and stopped housing joints, glued and pinned can be used for the purpose, and their use will result in a strong, well-made piece of furniture. If melamine-covered chipboard is chosen care is necessary if efficient joints are to be obtained.

Before concerning ourselves in detail with the joints, let us first see how a unit can be planned and made. Figure 24.1 is a pictorial view of a wall unit made from timber either 19 mm or 12 mm in thickness and up to 200 mm wide. The vertical sections in the unit should be approximately 600 mm wide and the shelves can be placed at any position to suit the objects which are to be placed on them.

One of the most important things in producing a unit so that it will remain square and in shape is to incorporate, somewhere, a cupboard of some sort—perhaps a drinks cupboard—so that a plywood back can be fitted. This piece of plywood will assist greatly in keeping the unit in shape. The small cupboard halfway-up and the three cupboards across the unit at floor level (figure 24.1) will enable one large and one small piece of 6 mm plywood to be fixed at the back to keep the unit rigid. Figure 24.2 shows how the plywood should be fitted; when secured an adhesive and brass screws should be used.

Figure 24.3 shows the toe space that has been provided across the lower part of the unit. In addition this illustration shows that the bottom shelf of the cupboards has been grooved to receive the top edge of the skirting, and that glue blocks have been fitted behind to give additional strength. The ends of the skirting have been recessed into the vertical pieces of the unit.

The door to the small cupboard on the right is in the form of a flap which is hinged on its bottom edge, preferably with a piano hinge (figure 24.4). This is a brass hinge that can be purchased in many lengths and should run the full width of the flap. The flap is held in the open position by a stay of which there are many forms. The stay shown in figure 24.1 is one example of these; another type has an arm in the form of a quadrant (a quarter circle). Care must be taken in fitting the stay to ensure that the door is able to open and close properly.

Now let us consider the joints to be used for fixing together the various components of the unit. Many of the units bought in shops

Figure 24.1

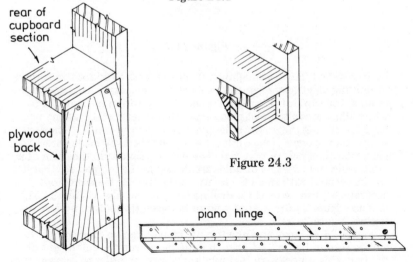

rear of
cupboard
section

plywood
back

Figure 24.2

Figure 24.3

piano hinge

Figure 24.4

W.—H

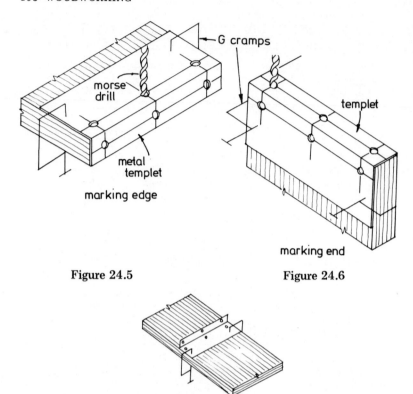

Figure 24.5   Figure 24.6

Figure 24.7

have dowelled joints throughout. If the reader is to adopt this form of jointing an efficient templet is absolutely necessary. A suggested templet for work of this nature is shown in position in figure 24.5, which illustrates a templet made from thin sheet metal that can be used for drilling the dowel holes accurately on the ends of boards as well as on the edges. Obviously, it has to be specially made for a particular thickness of material. The metal is shaped in the form of a right angle and two sets of holes are drilled in the templet so that it can be secured with small G cramps to the timber. If marked out accurately it can be used for drilling holes in the edge (figure 24.5), on end (figure 24.6), or at any point between the ends of a piece of timber (figure 24.7).

Figure 24.8 shows how the top of the unit can be marked out. It will be seen in figure 24.1 that the side pieces run the full height of the unit; this is necessary if chipboard is used, in order to prevent the cut ends of the crosspieces from being seen.

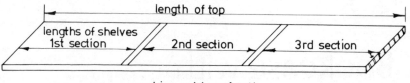

marking out top of unit

Figure 24.8

Figure 24.9

If it is decided not to use dowelled joints in the work, an alternative is to make very shallow stopped housing joints (say, 3 mm in depth), glued and nailed together. This necessitates nailing through the face of the chipboard, thus detracting from the appearance of the work. This can be overcome to a certain extent by carefully drilling shallow holes, through which the nails will be driven, in the face of the chipboard. The joint is secured with glue and nails and each of the holes is then filled with a plastics plug similar to that shown in figure 24.9. The reader should make sure that he can purchase these plugs before he embarks on the preparation of this type of joint.

25
Bookcase with Sliding Doors

The widespread interest in purchasing and reading books makes a bookcase in the home a necessary item. The bookcase illustrated in figure 25.1 is made from solid timber. The reader need not, of course, restrict himself to the use of solid timber; however, since it is better that the top and bottom tracks for the sliding glass doors be recessed into those parts of the casing to which they are adjacent, solid timber is the best of the choices available.

Figure 25.2 represents a vertical section through the bookcase and shows that it has two spaces for books. If additional shelving is required the dimensions of the case must be increased.

First of all, the four sides of the case should be made; if the top is required to overlap the sides, stopped housings should be used. The joints between the sides and the bottom of the case should be fairly strong so it is best to use a lapped, dovetailed joint at each of the corners. An alternative to the dovetailed joint is the stopped, tongued and grooved joint shown in figure 25.3.

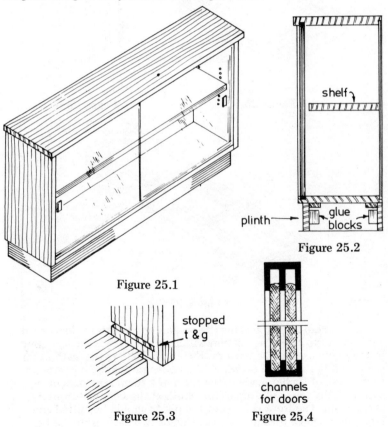

Figure 25.1

Figure 25.2

Figure 25.3

Figure 25.4

Grooves should be made in the top and bottom components to receive the tracks for the sliding glass doors. Remember to fit the deeper of the two tracks at the top so the glass doors can be placed and removed when necessary. The glass doors should overlap slightly when they are in the closed position and their height should be measured from the bottom of the grooves in the lower track to about 3 mm above the lower edge of the top track. The space above the doors will allow them to be lifted out when necessary (see figure 25.4).

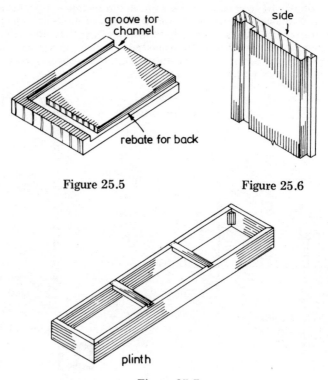

Figure 25.5   Figure 25.6

Figure 25.7

Figures 25.5 and 25.6 show the preparation necessary for the sides and top of the case. The bottom will have to be prepared according to the joints used at the bottom. Figure 25.7 shows the method for constructing the plinth on which the bookcase stands. It comprises four pieces of timber made in the form of a frame, the sizes being such that the case will overlap the plinth at the sides and front by, say, 25 mm. The front corners of the plinth should be mitred and butt joints can be used at the rear. One or two battens should be jointed to the longer sides of the plinth to give it more stability, and the corner joints can be strengthened with glue blocks. Small pieces of plywood should be glued and pinned to the bottom surface of the case at appropriate points so that the case can be positioned correctly on the plinth.

Small rectangular pieces of polished glass can be glued to the doors to act as handles, using a clear glue suitable for this type of work. Alternatively, the supplier of the glass doors can be asked to make recesses in the appropriate positions to act as finger grips.

Figure 25.6 shows that the sides to the bookcase are recessed in a similar way to the top and bottom components so that the tracks for the glass doors can be recessed out of sight. It is not absolutely necessary to have tracks down each side of the case, but they are a means of keeping the inside of the case dust free.

If blockboard is used for the manufacture of the bookcase, remember to lip the front edges of the pieces, especially if the work is not to be covered with laminated plastics. Also in this case, it is not necessary to recess the fibre tracks into the woodwork. These can be secured to the sides, top and bottom surfaces with a good contact adhesive.

26

Blanket Chest

Housewives with plenty of bed linen and blankets, items which take up a lot of space in cupboards, will welcome a present in the form of a blanket chest. This will enable them to store blankets as well as other bulky articles. Figure 26.1 shows a pictorial view of a chest with sides consisting of four panelled frames. The chest can be a very attractive addition to the home if made from a timber such as quarter-sawn oak, polished to show the wood's natural characteristics.

Figure 26.2 represents a vertical section through the chest and shows that the top is a solid piece of timber moulded around its edges. The two sides seen in the drawing have what are called fielded and raised panels. The bottom of the chest is secured to the lower edges of the frames and a skirting has been secured around the base.

Figure 26.3 shows how the setting out rod should be prepared. At (a) is the 'length' rod, which shows that the two long sides of the chest have three panels; (b), showing the end frame, demonstrates that the thicknesses of the two longer frames have to be deducted from the over-all width of the 'width' rod. At (c) is seen the 'height' rod; this shows the lid at the top, the bottom of the chest adjacent to the bottom rails of the frames, and the skirting that surrounds the lower edge of the chest.

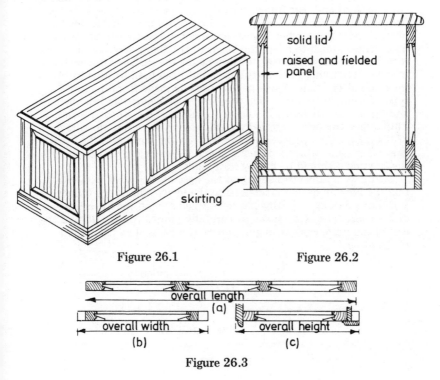

Figure 26.1   Figure 26.2

Figure 26.3

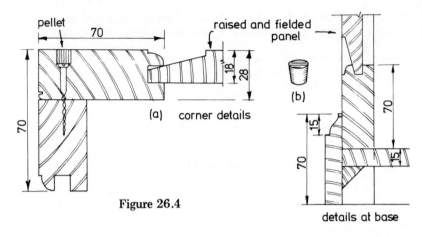

Figure 26.4

Figure 26.5

Figure 26.4 illustrates how the four sides of the chest are connected. The front and rear frames butt against the edges of the two end frames and are screwed together in this position. To enable one to obtain a neat finish when frames are screwed together in this way, holes large enough to allow the heads of the fixing screws to be sunk to a depth of approximately 10 mm below the surface must be bored in the longer frames. Pellets (figure 26.4b) can then be used to fill the holes after fixing. These pellets must be made from the same type of wood as that to which they are to be secured and the face grain (not the end grain) should be on the top edge of each pellet. Thus, when the pellet is glued into its hole in the frame the direction of the grain of the pellet should be exactly the same as that of the component into which it is being glued. When cleaned off flush with the framing it should be hardly noticeable.

Figure 26.5 illustrates details at the base of the chest. It shows that the bottom has been screwed to the lower rails of the frames and that a moulded skirting has been fixed around the lower edges of the chest. The skirting can be carefully pinned to the rails and the end of the framework, and glue blocks can be used to strengthen the jointing.

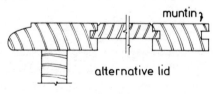

Figure 26.6

Figure 26.6 shows an alternative method for constructing the lid
of the chest. The lid consists of a panelled frame with muntins
introduced to break up the panelled area into smaller sections. The
panels are made to be flush with the top of the framing, as seen in
the drawing. The edges of the frame are moulded in a manner similar
to that used in making the solid top.

27

Semicircular Table

A semicircular table, the framing of which is illustrated in figure 27.1 is, contrary to popular belief, fairly easy to make. The most tedious part of the work to be done is making the means to manufacture the semicircular rail.

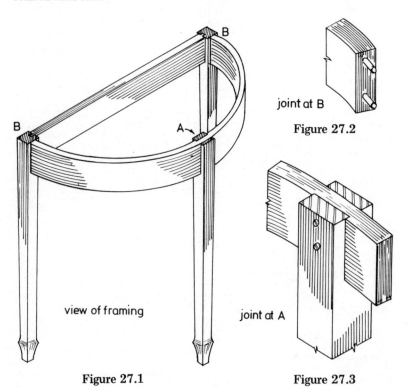

joint at B

Figure 27.2

view of framing

Figure 27.1

joint at A

Figure 27.3

The table consists of three legs (or four if desired), the shape of which can be produced on a overhand planing machine. Alternatively, they can be purchased at a local DIY store. Legs of some other design may perhaps be preferred to that shown in the figure.

The two rear legs are connected by a rail, say 100 × 25 mm. The joints can be morticed and tenoned, or dowelled (as seen in figure 27.2). The circular rail, which should also be around 100 × 25 mm, should also be secured to the rear legs by using the dowelled joint, and the front leg or legs connected to the curved rail by the method shown in figure 27.3. All the joints should be glued with a synthetic resin adhesive and that at the front should also be dowelled or screwed from the back (see figure 27.3).

Now let us turn to the manufacture of the semicircular rail. The rail is made from a number of layers of thin veneer of a timber matching the rest of the table. Veneers are fairly easy to obtain and 1–2 mm is the thickness to choose. It may be necessary to buy the veneer in the form of a sheet which will have to be cut to the width required for the rail (100 mm), using a straight edge and the point of a sharp knife. The number of veneers required will depend on the thickness of the veneers, that is, how many it takes to make up a thickness of 25 mm.

Having obtained the veneer the means of forming the rail to the correct shape must be made. First, a base board is required; this can be, say, 19 mm blockboard (figure 27.4). Then, using a trammel (figure 27.5) the shape of the rail should be set out on the base board. Blocks of wood should be prepared in the shapes on either

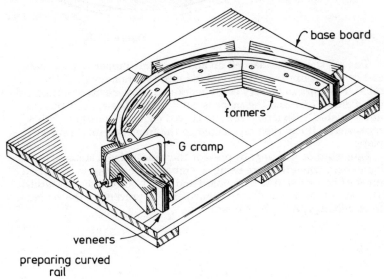

preparing curved
rail

Figure 27.4

side of the setting out (figure 27.4). The inner set should then be screwed very carefully to the inner curve of the rail.

The prepared veneers are then placed in position around the inner formers secured to the board and the outer formers are placed against them and cramped with G cramps to check that the thickness of the rail will be correct when the veneers are glued together. Having checked this, the veneers can be released from the formers and their surfaces—not, of course, the outside surfaces—glued with a resin glue such as Cascomite. The veneers should then be placed around the formers again, and, starting from one end, the outer formers should be positioned and cramped up tight. The veneers should be left for, say, twenty-four hours before finally being released from the formers.

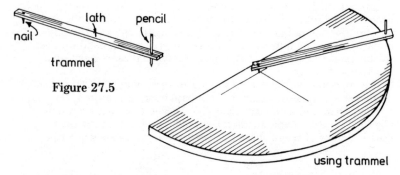

Figure 27.5

using trammel

Figure 27.6

The rail should be cleaned up and the joints prepared at its ends and centre. It can then be assembled into the framework of the table. The top can be very easily marked out by means of a trammel (see figure 27.6), and the shape is cut on a band saw, or, if this is not available, with a bow saw; its curved edge is cleaned up with a spokeshave. It can then be secured to the framing with shrinkage plates.

One word of warning: to prevent the veneers from sticking to the base board when they are being assembled, it is advisable to place a sheet of paper over the base board and to set out the shape on this. The rail is then assembled on the paper thus preventing the veneer from adhering to the base board.

28

Chest of Drawers

A chest of drawers is likely to be a very popular addition to the home—not the large, bulky kind used for storing bed linen, but the more elegant type which can be placed in a lounge and used for storing papers and similar items. When made in the traditional style from a wood such as mahogany this can be a most attractive piece of furniture of which the owner can be proud.

Figure 28.1 shows a small chest of drawers and suggested dimensions for the width and depth are given. The height of the chest should be around 1 m but this of course depends on the width and depth plus the number of the drawers it contains.

Figure 28.2 represents a pictorial view of the carcassing that the work requires. The two sides are of solid timber, but veneered block-board can be used if so desired. The sides are rebated at the rear to receive the 6 mm plywood back. Rails, 50 × 25 mm either dowelled or twin-morticed and tenoned to the sides, separate the drawers. In line with the rails are fixed the runners to the drawers. These should be of timber, around 25 × 18 mm. The feet to the chest should be shaped as shown in the two drawings, the side effect being obtained by shaping the lower ends of the sides of the chest. The front shapes have to be made separately and are jointed to the chest as seen in figure 28.2 and in more detail in figures 28.3a and b.

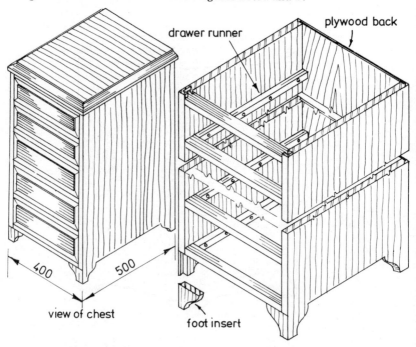

drawer runner

plywood back

400

500

view of chest

foot insert

Figure 28.1   Figure 28.2

The rail across the front of the chest at the top should be dove-tailed to the sides to ensure that there is sufficient strength in the cabinet at this position. A larger detail of this joint is shown in figure 28.4. The dovetail is recessed into the top edge to a sufficient depth to allow the sides also to be recessed into the top of the chest. Details of the preparation of the top are given in figure 28.5. This drawing shows that the back edge has been stop-rebated, to receive the plywood back, and also grooved, to receive the top edges of the sides of the cabinet. In addition, the top has been moulded around three of its edges to match the moulding on the drawer fronts.

Figure 28.6 gives suggested dimensions for the mouldings around the top and the fronts of the drawers. Figure 28.7 shows, in two stages, how these mouldings can be prepared using simple hand tools. In (a) is seen the first step, which consists of rebating around the edges to be moulded to a depth of 3 mm. The bevelled portion of the mouldings can be made with a shoulder plane or a badger plane, whichever is available (figure 28.9b).

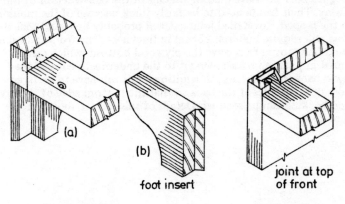

(a)

(b)

foot insert

joint at top of front

Figure 28.3

Figure 28.4

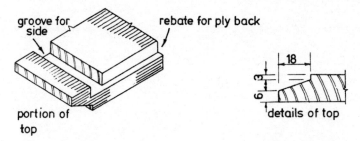

groove for side

rebate for ply back

portion of top

18

3

6

details of top

Figure 28.5

Figure 28.6

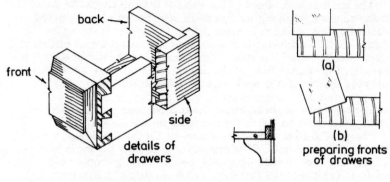

back

front

side

details of
drawers

(a)

(b)
preparing fronts
of drawers

Figure 28.7   **Figure 28.8**   **Figure 28.9**

Figure 28.7 provides pictorial details of the construction of the drawers. Their fronts need to be fairly thick because of the moulding and the lapped, dovetailed joints; it will probably be found that the fronts will require material 25 mm in thickness. The fronts and sides should be grooved to receive the plywood bottom, which can be secured in position by screwing it to the underneath edge of the drawer back. Incidentally, an additional rail will have to be fixed across the two sides at the back so that the bottom edge of the plywood backing can be secured. Details of this rail are shown in figure 28.8.

29
Tool Box

If one is to purchase a kit of woodworking tools—which will
certainly cost a considerable sum of money—it is natural to want to
protect them. The best way to do this is to make a tool box in which
the tools can be stored in an orderly and accessible way. Figure 29.1
shows a pictorial view of a tool box with its lid in the open position
revealing removable trays for small tools situated near to the top.
Figure 29.2 represents a section through the box and shows that it
has four of these trays; figure 29.3 shows how they are supported in
the box.

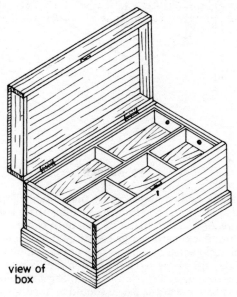

view of
box

Figure 29.1

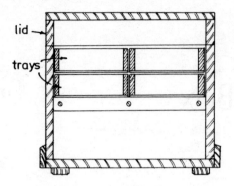

Figure 29.2

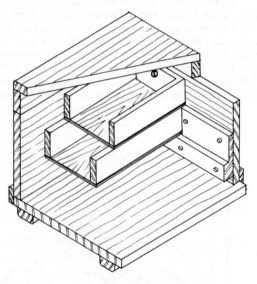

Figure 29.3

The box can be made quite easily by first obtaining the four sides and the top and bottom, and gluing and nailing these together as shown in figure 29.4. Solid timber 25 mm in thickness is best for this, but 19 mm blockboard can be substituted if necessary.

A synthetic resin adhesive such as Cascomite and 50 mm oval brads should be used in the assembly. When the six pieces have been assembled, the corners and top and bottom edges should be smoothed with a plane and a marking gauge should be used for marking a line around the four sides equal to the depth of the lid of the box

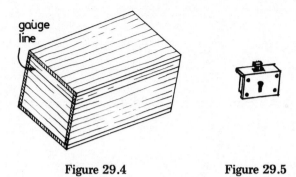

Figure 29.4   **Figure 29.5**

(around 80 mm). When this has been done a panel saw should be used for cutting around the gauge mark, thus producing a lid exactly the same size as the lower part of the box. The two cut edges should then be cleaned with a smoothing plane, checking, when this has been done, that the two parts fit closely together and adjusting if necessary. The lid portion can be used for storing the saws in the kit.

Battens should be glued and screwed to the underneath surface of the box to keep it off the ground, and a strip of timber—say, 75 × 12 mm—can be mitred around the lower edge of the box, this being only to make the box more attractive in appearance. The lid should be hinged to the lower section with two 62 mm brass hinges and a brass hook-type lock should be fitted near to the centre of the front (see figure 29.5).

The trays rest on supports screwed to the inside surfaces of the ends of the box and are made from 12 mm timber, glued and nailed together with as many divisions as required. The 6 mm plywood bottom can also be glued and screwed into position. The depths of the trays can be anything from 50 mm to 75 mm, and 25 mm holes are cut at both ends of each tray for easy removal.

Saws (a hand saw and a tenon saw) can be stored in the lid, together with a square (see figure 4.9). This square is likely to prove to be very useful on occasions and is very simple to make. Its size should allow it to fit into the lid of the box.